PASS YOUR ADVANCED MOTORCYCLING TEST

PASS YOUR ADVANCED
MOTORCYCLING TEST

PUBLISHED IN ASSOCIATION WITH THE
INSTITUTE OF ADVANCED MOTORISTS

Published 1996 by
Bay View Books Ltd
The Red House
25-26 Bridgeland Street
Bideford
Devon EX39 2PZ

Reprinted 1997
Reprinted 1998

Edited by Mark Hughes
Text consultancy by Rod Collins
Photography by Kerry Dunlop
Designed by Bruce Aiken
Typeset by Sarah Ward

ISBN 1 870979 65 6
Printed in Great Britain
by Butler & Tanner,
Frome, Somerset

ACKNOWLEDGEMENTS
Grateful thanks are due to our
featured riders: Carol Boydell
(Honda VFR750F), Rod Collins
(BMW R100 GS), John Cordner
(Honda Fireblade CBR900 RR),
Hilary Day (Honda Fireblade
CBR900 RR), Derek Grove
(Yamaha FZR1000 EXUP), Danny
Thompson (Honda Fireblade
CBR900 RR) and Roger Wilcox
(Honda CBR1000 FK). Other
help with photography came
from Peter Avard, Terry Collins,
Paul Hardiman, John Callan (of
The Shout Picture Company),
James Mann, Transport Research
Laboratory, BMW (GB) Ltd,
Green Flag National Breakdown,
Andrews Professional Colour
Laboratories Ltd (Ashford, Kent),
The Foundry (Canterbury, Kent),
The Bike Shop (Faversham,
Kent) and Guymark UK.

How to use this book

This book is designed to be used both for self-study and to supplement expert tuition. The way it is organised in themes and topics allows you quickly to find the information you need, so that you can refer to it regularly as you develop individual areas of your motorcycling technique. The most important topics are conveniently summarised at the end of each chapter under the headings 'Advanced checklist' and 'What the examiner looks for'. When you have absorbed and practised all the skills, you should be able to pass the Advanced Motorcycling Test with ease. Improving your technique, however, is a never-ending process, so remember to use this book to brush up on your skills throughout your motorcycling career.

Pass Your Advanced Motorcycling Test

Contents

4 ADVANCED RIDING IN DIFFICULT CONDITIONS

5 ADVANCED MOTORWAY RIDING

6 ADVANCED ADVICE FOR YOUR RIDING CAREER

7 THE ADVANCED MOTORCYCLING TEST

1 PRINCIPLES OF ADVANCED MOTORCYCLING

What is advanced motorcycling?

Quiet efficiency: the hallmark of the expert

Advanced riders are unobtrusive. All kinds of traffic and road conditions are dealt with quietly and efficiently. You do not see flashes of brake lights like a disco show laser or hear peak revs in all the gears. Yet they always seem to be ahead of the game. There are always gaps in the traffic just when required, the lights always seem to go green just as these riders roll up to the line, and really you hardly notice their presence before they are safely away out of sight on the open road.

Advanced riders are always unobtrusive: you hardly notice their presence before they are safely away out of sight.

Knee-scraping 'sports' riders will often make short-term progress ahead of the advanced rider, but most of the time their more spectacular antics will leave them boxed in behind a traffic queue, or they will force other drivers to brake hard to let them in after optimistic overtaking. And while they might gain a mile or two by these tactics, on a cross-country journey you can guarantee the advanced rider will average a better speed and arrive much fresher.

A fringe benefit of riding to an advanced level is less wear and tear on your machine. Brakes do not need new pads so often and tyres last longer.

There is another important spin-off. Anything we can do to show the motorcyclist in a more positive light in the eyes of other road users is worthwhile. The quiet efficiency our rider displays will not ruffle the feathers of car drivers stuck in traffic. A friendly wave as a gap opens up gives a good impression, far removed from the stereotyped images.

With the media still epitomising motorcyclists as 'Hells Angels', and the phrase 'roaring down the road' still regularly trotted out, we need to restore the balance by adopting good riding skills.

Advanced riding is fun

Mention of advanced riding might conjure up visions of boring old blokes on BMWs, but this picture is out of date. Enthusiasm for motorcycling, not age, sex or choice of machine, is what unites riders who develop their skills to the level required to pass the Advanced Motorcycling Test conducted by the Institute of Advanced Motorists.

At any gathering of IAM riders you will find plenty of superbikes: Fireblades, GSX 1100s, FZRs and the odd Ducati or Guzzi. True, BMWs will be around too, but they will not be a majority. Chances are there will be a few Gold Wings, perhaps a Harley or two, and even a classic from the days when British bikes reigned supreme. Lower capacity sports bikes will also be there.

Advanced motorcycling appeals to young, sporting riders as well as mature ones, some of whom may be returning to two wheels after a long lapse. Whatever a rider's background and preference, advanced techniques and application of roadcraft, as practised by police motorcycle patrols, will make life on our crowded roads safer and more enjoyable.

Advanced riders with advanced bikes – a couple of best-selling Fireblades.

The need for advanced riding

Safe control of a superbike with race-level performance demands advanced skills.

The standard of training in the UK for new motorcyclists has never been higher and rider casualties are falling. Learners must now undergo Compulsory Basic Training before being allowed unaccompanied on the road. The regulations have spawned a large number of training organisations, some of which also offer advanced training for qualified riders.

This is all good news, but the need for motorcyclists, especially young ones, to develop advanced skills has never been greater. Traffic conditions are more demanding than ever before and most accidents still involve less experienced riders of low-capacity machines.

Many drivers have no conception of a motorcyclist's problems, such as the effects of poor surfaces. The gains in car performance – as well as safety features like anti-lock brakes and traction control – can induce drivers to travel faster and leave less braking distance.

All this makes it more difficult for the average rider to stay out of trouble, and emphasises the need for defensive motorcycle roadcraft. To be fair to car drivers, similar advances in superbike design also encourage a few riders to explore the limits, leaving little margin for error.

In recent years spectacular leaps in motorcycle technology have occurred, such as computer-controlled fuel injection and ignition, ABS braking and heads with four or five valves per cylinder. Some manufacturers have developed radically different suspension layouts, moving away at last from the traditional tele-fork front end. Tyres, too, have reached levels of stability and adhesion that could not be imagined 10 years ago.

Race-level performance from production machines is available to any rider who can afford to buy and run one. So there is all the more need for riders to learn advanced riding techniques to match the advanced technology.

Higher riding standards also have a part to play in countering threats to the pleasure of motorcycling. EC legislation may eventually limit engine output to 100bhp despite the absence of any proof that a significant proportion of accidents result from riders using high-powered machines.

Environmentally friendly

Advanced machinery: blue BMW R1100 with tele-lever front end and red Yamaha GTS1000 with hub centre steering.

Motorcycling is often seen as a leisure activity these days, but many people use low-capacity machines as daily transport. Consider the environmental advantages of the two-wheeler: its minimal use of road space, potential economy and contribution to relieving traffic congestion are just a few.

It is sad, then, that the government offers no incentives to motorcyclists, unlike owners of classic cars, when motor taxation inevitably rises with each budget. And have you ever heard of a motorcycle causing a motorway pile-up?

Comfort and safety

Riding position

Comfort and safety start with your riding position. You should sit in a natural position, with your body leaning forward slightly and your hands able to reach the controls comfortably. Your feet should remain in the correct position at all times so that you can operate the gearchange and rear brake swiftly in an emergency.

Do not be tempted to emulate the semi-prone position used by racing stars. It is completely inappropriate on the road, compromising control of your machine, reducing your ability to observe the conditions around you and leading to extra fatigue. If you find yourself trying to 'streamline' your body in order to tease a little more speed from your motorcycle, you are either riding too fast or need a more powerful machine.

Sit in a natural position (above), with your body leaning slightly forward. A semi-prone 'racing' position (right) compromises your control.

The need for good clothing

Motorcycling clothes must possess four main qualities: they must keep the rider warm, dry, conspicuous and protected in the event of an accident. All this must be achieved without causing any discomfort or impairing ability to operate the controls.

When considering clothing, not every rider seeks the same comfort and safety. As there are so many different ways of fulfilling these aims, your type of use needs to be your first thought.

If you tend to cover short distances on a motorcycle equipped with a fairing, the good protection it offers will mean that a lightweight anorak or oversuit should normally be adequate. At the other end of the scale, long winter journeys on a large-capacity superbike will be covered most comfortably in three layers of clothing: a top layer to keep out water, a second to keep you warm and a third to give protection in the event of an accident.

Most riders happily settle for less expensive and elaborate clothing for everyday use, but need an outfit which is good enough to get them through an occasional winter cross-country trip. Everyone has different views on how this can be achieved. To work out the balance which suits you, obtain a general idea from the following section describing the main groups of clothing available, and then see for yourself what the various manufacturers offer. But avoid too much of a compromise: serious motorcycling definitely demands high-quality clothing.

As well as being comfortable and protected, you need to be conspicuous. A driver failing to see a motorcyclist is a major factor in about one-third of all accidents involving motorcycles, and the proportion is highest around town in daylight. The bright, modern clothes now available certainly help you to be seen, and many incorporate reflective material as part of their styling. If you already own dark clothing you can add a red or yellow 'dayglo' waistcoat or a fluorescent belt of Sam Browne pattern with a diagonal strap over the shoulder.

Protecting yourself

Research has shown that 85 per cent of accidents resulting in injury to motorcyclists involve frontal or near-frontal impacts in which the rider is usually thrown off his bike.

Conventional wisdom has always suggested that a motorcyclist about to have an accident should 'step off' his machine, since the chances of escaping serious injury are better if you are sliding along the road rather than rolling with the bike likely to land on top of you. Whether you abandon ship or are thrown clear, scraping along the road will certainly cause minor injuries unless you are well protected.

The legal obligation to wear a helmet means that your head is looked after, but hands, feet, arms and legs are vulnerable, especially if you land awkwardly. However warm the weather, you need to wear gloves, boots and a tough jacket as a minimum.

While you work to develop the skills of advanced riding to a level which ensures that you will never be involved in an accident, do recognise that you need to be dressed for protection. Try to buy the best and most durable equipment you can afford.

Impact protectors for elbows, knees and body.

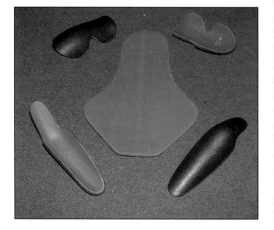

Choosing your clothing

The oldest answer to the problem of keeping out wind and rain is still quite effective – the two-piece waxed cotton oversuit. Introduced originally by Barbour but now widely imitated, these garments are still the only choice for many motorcyclists.

A four-pocket jacket reaching to the hips and elastic-waisted trousers are good at keeping out water, and retain warmth reasonably well. However, the material does need reproofing from time to time. It amuses older motorcyclists, who were accustomed to being barred from pubs because their protective clothing made the chairs greasy, that nowadays the Barbour jacket has become the uniform of the green-wellied set.

This type of two-piece suit, sometimes called a trials suit, is also made in nylon. While this material is cheaper and more stylish for some tastes, it is not as effective as waxed cotton, but trials suits are reasonably convenient and very good at keeping out cold and damp. Some have a detachable lining that can be removed in summer.

Although similar to a trials suit, the continental suit usually has a shorter jacket with elastic in the waist, and higher-waisted trousers held up by braces. The many variations in style, fastenings and pockets all provide good draught-proofing from the tight waist. A bonus for some riders is that the jackets look smart when worn on their own. The more lightweight continental suits are often bought to be worn both on and off the bike, but might not provide enough winter warmth.

Before choosing from all the styles, colours, weights and lining thicknesses of continental

or trials suits, consider your needs – the proportion of long and short journeys you will cover in winter and summer – and buy a suit which will fit over your other clothes.

These same considerations apply to one-piece suits, which are available in waxed cotton, nylon or other plastics. There are heavy-duty and lined versions, together with lightweight types suitable as a waterproof layer over other clothes. One-piece suits tend to look bulky when you are walking around as they have enough material in the seat to allow knees and back to be bent when you are riding. They are usually as warm as more expensive two-piece equivalents,

The top of the range in leather suits: specially treated leather means that BMW's Atlantis suit always remains waterproof.

Suits in bright colours are stylish as well as conspicuous.

piece oversuit may also be needed for wet weather, while winter conditions may require something heavier as well.

BMW has produced the first waterproof leather suit, using specially treated leather. If you can justify the Atlantis suit's high price, you need look no further.

New-generation suits incorporating waterproof 'Goretex' are as expensive as most leather suits but much more versatile. For the first time, motorcyclists (as well as climbers and others who require outdoor protection) have a material available which guarantees 100 per cent impermeability, yet can breathe so that condensation and perspiration are prevented. Use of this wonder fabric now extends to gloves and mittens, and even liners for leather boots. If money is no object, it is possible to remain comfortable and dry from fingertips to toes.

Summing up the suit situation, a lined two-piece is probably the best answer for serious winter riding. For local commuting, where you perhaps have a train or bus alternative in the worst weather, an anorak and plastic over-trousers should be sufficient. Between these extremes choose the compromise which best meets your needs and pocket: you will probably end up with combinations of suits which can be used with tee-shirts and pullovers to deal with a variety of conditions. Whatever you choose, check that the details – zips, Velcro strips, pockets, waterproof flaps, seam linings, colour, style – suit your taste and seem capable of withstanding hard use.

Always wear gloves, for protection in an accident as well as keeping warm. Thin, unlined leather gloves provide the most comfort and best control in hot

weather; lined leather gloves or mittens (mittens are generally warmer than gloves) should cope with colder conditions; and in wet weather waxed cotton or plastic over-mittens on top of lined or unlined gloves are best.

When dressing yourself up for winter riding, take care not to end up with so many layers of material over your hands that you have difficulty in feeling and operating the controls – but remember that frozen fingers are not very sensitive either.

To keep your neck warm and dry where helmet and collar meet, wear a woollen or silk scarf, or a 'tube' or balaclava (particularly useful items when using an open-face helmet) made of wool, cotton or silk.

Strong shoes or boots are essential. As well as leaving your feet vulnerable in an accident, ordinary shoes or trainers will make them cold and wet in rain, and the upper part of the left shoe will soon disintegrate against the gear-shift. Durable leather boots and thick woollen socks are the answer for many riders, but untreated leather starts to let in water after an hour's riding. Winter boots incorporating 'Goretex' are another answer. For a long journey in rain, waxed cotton,

but they take more time to put on and take off. Most riders who use one-piece suits acknowledge that they cannot always keep out all water on a long journey in hard rain, but they can still prove very effective when worn with suitable clothes underneath.

Among the more expensive options are one-piece or two-piece leather suits, which are durable, comfortable and stylish. For the riders who choose them, however, their greatest advantage is their resistance to abrasion, which appeals to anyone conscious of the fact that they may one day find themselves sliding along a road. You can buy a leather suit off the peg or made to measure: in either case, look for a snug fit to prevent billowing in a one-piece and draughts in a two-piece, and make sure that the sleeves are long enough.

Remember that leather is not the best material for keeping out the cold and will not remain waterproof for more than an hour or so in rain. A thin one-

Two-piece suits can be more versatile, but the jacket must fit snugly enough to prevent draughts.

A selection of touring boots, which are usually black.

High-quality leather gloves with extra knuckle and finger protection.

plastic or rubber over-shoes are reasonably effective.

Dispatch riders, and others who cover long distances in all weathers, resort to another aid to riding comfort: electrically heated gloves, socks and waistcoats. For one IAM member who thinks nothing of riding from London to Edinburgh and back on a 24-hour business trip, electrically heated clothing makes bearable hundreds of miles in wintry conditions which otherwise could not be tolerated. For less dedicated motorcyclists, electrically heated grips are a good choice for cold weather.

Helmets

Chin protection is cleverly hinged on a BMW System 3 helmet.

A top-of-the-range full-face helmet made by Arai.

An FM full-face, costing about half the price of the most expensive helmets.

Jet-style Shoei helmet is among the best open-face choices.

fits well. The snuggest fit which will cause no discomfort, even during a long journey, is what you should aim for.

All helmets on the British market offer the necessary level of protection because they have to survive stringent testing in the laboratories of the British Standards Institution. The helmet you buy will withstand repeated blows, resist penetration by sharp objects and have a strong enough strap to cope with the most severe impacts.

The conventional materials used for the shells of motorcycle helmets are GRP (glass-reinforced plastics, commonly called glass-fibre), polycarbonate and ABS. The advent of high-tech materials such as Kevlar and carbon-fibre has meant that they are often incorporated in the shell construction, but seem to be more of a sales aid than a technical necessity.

Glass-fibre is still considered to be among the best, although it is more expensive than polycarbonate and somewhat heavier. Polycarbonate is entirely adequate for everyday use as opposed to racing, but it does

Shapes vary and sizes are inconsistent between one manufacturer and another, so take plenty of time and keep trying on different helmets of your chosen type and price range until you find the one which fits best. A helmet costing £200 and made to the highest standards will not protect you properly in an accident unless it become brittle with age and needs to be replaced after a few years. Unlike a glass-fibre helmet, a polycarbonate plastic one must never be painted or covered with stickers because it can be weakened by some solvents and chemicals.

The two types respond differently on impact. Glass-fibre flexes to absorb energy and then starts to break up so that it will show marks after a crash. Polycarbonate plastic deforms elastically and reverts to its original shape so that no damage shows. Any helmet, therefore, should be replaced after a very hard impact, even if there is no visible sign of damage.

Some authorities recommend that a helmet should be replaced after four years' use, since slight weakening occurs with age and exposure to the elements. This may seem extravagant, especially if you find an old helmet comfortable, but ask yourself how much importance you attach to your head – probably a fair bit.

Your helmet, needless to say, should also be looked after carefully so that it never drops on to the ground or comes into contact with damaging chemicals or solvents.

Besides choice of material, you need to choose between full-face or open-face styles. Full-face (or integral) helmets offer better face and chin protection in an accident and excellent weather protection in normal riding, but some riders find them claustrophobic to wear and prefer the more traditional open-face style. Full-face helmets can also be lifted uncomfortably by the wind at high speed, and they tend to be more expensive.

Straps, visors and goggles

Strap fastenings need to be easy to use because it is irritating to struggle with them every time you put your helmet on and take it off. Check the ease of adjustment if the helmet is to be used by more than one person – by a pillion passenger, for example – to remove the risk of someone wearing it insecurely.

Chin straps are normally made of nylon, but leather is also used. If the wearer of a helmet has a chin cup fitted, it is now a legal – and safety – requirement that this cup is worn on a secondary chin strap, which will have to be added if the helmet has only one strap.

Good eye protection is vital. Riding with neither visor nor goggles is extremely foolish, since road grit, stones or glass can be thrown into your eyes by other traffic even when riding slowly over a short distance. Goggles and visors need to keep out draughts and be durable. Scuffs and scratches reduce your vision, particularly at night.

It is worth buying the best possible equipment, as good lenses, whether in glass or polycarbonate, are less likely to become scratched. Goggles should have a BS4110 rating of '2A', so avoid any on the market, such as ski-type goggles, which do not meet this specification.

Look after visors and goggles carefully: sponging them with warm, soapy water will keep them scrupulously clean. Avoid wiping them with gloved fingers while on the road in wet weather because you may scratch the surface. Water should be blown off a clean surface, but, if you do have difficulty with vision, stop and clean the visor or goggles properly.

The detachable peaks and visors made for open-face helmets are quite effective as sun-shields and air deflectors in town, but they tend to be lifted badly by wind pressure when riding at higher speeds.

Hearing protection

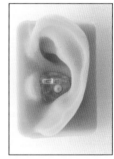

The various ways of protecting hearing range from simple ear plugs to ear mouldings made-to-measure by Guymark.

Recent research on the effect of speed on noise levels inside motorcycle helmets has focused attention on hearing protection. Noise levels can be much higher than the maximum safety limit of 90dB, and each doubling of speed increases noise by 16dB. It is believed that alterations to design will not necessarily cure the problem.

What this means to you as an advanced motorcyclist, probably accustomed to using the performance of your machine, is that you must take steps to protect your hearing. Use ear plugs or a similar type of ear defence. Some police forces are so concerned about the effects of high-speed noise that they test their patrolmen regularly for hearing loss, and take off patrol duty any rider whose hearing shows significant deterioration.

Security

An advanced motorcyclist tends to own the sort of motorcycle which is particularly attractive to criminals – joyriders, twinners, ringers or dealers in stolen parts.

The term 'joyrider' is a misnomer. A significant proportion of fatal accidents involve youngsters who steal machines 'just for a laugh' and abandon them later, probably the same evening. Where is the joy for friends and family left behind, or for the owner of the wrecked bike?

A twinner steals a motorcycle similar to his own and then fits the number plates from his original, damaged bike. A ringer is much more professional: he may buy a wreck to obtain legitimate documentation before stealing an identical model in order to switch the Vehicle Identification Number (VIN) plate and other identifying marks.

Superbikes or parts and accessories from them are often stolen to order. Many end up on the race track, where there is less risk of a spot check. The motor sport arena, sadly, is an obvious market for stolen property since there is a constant need to replace worn-out or damaged parts.

Some of the motorcycle security devices that can be found at a good dealer.

You are at greater risk if your motorcycle is a race replica or a sports model. It is important to recognise which kinds of criminal might be attracted to your machine so that you can fit appropriate security. There are four main types of product.

Alarms are usually activated by inertia or shock sensors, but sometimes the bike is protected by a cocoon of microwaves. The better types tend to be adjustable for sensitivity. The best will sound even if there is an attempt to remove just one component. It is false economy to choose a cheap alarm which might activate frequently as there is a strong temptation to leave it switched off.

Immobilisers break the ignition circuit, which can only be completed again by using the dedicated jackplug. Since these are passive devices they are less embarrassing than a noisy alarm, but they will not prevent your motorcycle being carried away in a van.

Physical security devices include padlocks with chains or armoured cable, U-shackles, disc locks and wheel clamps. Any of these is a strong visible deterrent, especially if the bike is attached to something fixed. But bolt croppers can overcome all but the strongest chain, so render them less effective by fitting the chain as high as possible on the bike.

Security marking may take the form of postcodes or other identification marks etched into various parts of the bike, or maybe a more sophisticated system whereby microchips are implanted in hollow parts of the machine. In either case it is imperative that prominent labels indicate that security marking exists, although this system is more effective in tracing a stolen bike than in preventing a theft.

A combination of all four methods is obviously the most effective. Given time, an expert thief can overcome most security measures. All we can hope to do is to force the criminal to take more time, make more noise or be more conspicuous. The golden rule is to buy the best you can afford.

Some of the best security costs nothing. The risk of theft depends more on where you leave your machine than anything else. Clearly your bike is safest when it is locked away, hidden from view in a secure garage, preferably shackled to an eyebolt set in the concrete floor, and alarmed.

If you must leave your machine unattended outside, try to ensure that it is in full view of as many passers-by as possible, under a street light if it is dark. A motorcycle is most vulnerable when it is left in the same place each day for a lengthy period, usually overnight at home or during the day while its owner is at work.

Thinking ahead

Why you need to think ahead

All road users need to adopt a planned and systematic approach to handling their vehicles, but this is doubly important for the motorcyclist.

When you concentrate on the conditions around you and anticipate what lies ahead, every manoeuvre can be carried out in good time and under complete control. Experience improves a rider's skill in planning his actions, but the need to concentrate and anticipate must never be underestimated.

Although a motorcycle is very stable when moving, there is a delicate balance of forces acting on it. If this balance is suddenly disturbed, the machine will fall over and take you with it. The best way to remain upright and in complete control is to avoid sudden changes in the relationship between road surface and tyres – fierce braking, hard acceleration, bad gearchanging or sudden changes of direction. Think ahead so that each change of condition is made smoothly and gradually.

Anticipation and concentration, necessary at all times, become vital at complex junctions.

Riding plans

At the very heart of the theory of advanced motorcycling technique is the riding plan. How information is assessed and acted upon distinguishes the truly advanced rider from the novice.

The riding plan is based on three questions:

1   What can be seen?
2   What cannot be seen?
3   What may be reasonably expected to happen?

Riding plans must be based on what is actually observed, and the assumptions that there may be danger in every obscured section of road and that others may do something foolish at any moment.

It is rare to be able to base your riding plans purely on what you can see, because there are nearly always obscured areas. There may be a bend to the right, a blind junction, a hump-back bridge or a high-sided vehicle – any of these can impede your view. Try as you might to extend your view round hazards, ultimately you have to decide to ride within the limits of what you can see, expecting any threat lurking in those concealed areas.

Imagine a typical B-road with tall hedges. You are following a car and want to overtake as soon as you get a good view. There is a series of bends ahead, first to the right then to the left. Even when you

position well to the left to obtain the earliest view, that offside section never truly opens up. To overtake with that danger area present would be suicidal, since a low sports car or perhaps another motorcyclist could be lurking there somewhere, unobserved.

The third question – what may reasonably be expected to happen? – is the one that catches out the inexperienced rider, and it calls for skilful interpretation of the visual clues. Still on that B-road, you have an advanced warning triangle for a bend to the left. In the road ahead you see grass trimmings along the nearside edge. What do you do?

Well, what can you see? A bend ahead, but you cannot yet

A riding plan in town: safely passing this lorry requires awareness of stationary traffic ahead, the oncoming flow in the distance, the parked car on the right and the possibility of pedestrians appearing between vehicles.

Imagine you are commentary riding: you would notice the Pelican crossing, people waiting at the right, the density of traffic, the road ahead bending to the left, and the limited visibility beyond the bus.

see round it. You can see the grass in the road, so you can expect a hedge trimmer operating just around the bend, blocking half the road. So before you smell the newly-cut grass, you will have adjusted your speed to negotiate the bend, fully prepared to slow down or stop. Vehicles might be behind you, so give a 'slow down' signal if required.

Similarly, you might be following a commercial vehicle. Make a mental note of what kind it is. If it is a bread van, and you can see shops ahead, expect it to be making a delivery there, possibly without signalling and in the most awkward place.

The same goes for a bus or coach. If you persist in following closely so that you cannot see

when a stop is coming up, you may get stuck behind it when it picks up passengers. You will have only yourself to blame. If you stay well back, looking out for stops, and anticipate the inevitability of the bus stopping, you will be ready to overtake as soon as the road is clear.

At night accurate observation is even more important, but different clues are available. Physical clues may be few in the diminished light, but the presence and position of other vehicles may be indicated by their headlights. By day they would not be seen until emerging from that side turning, but at night you receive advanced warning.

When practising your riding plans, never assume anything.

ASSUME: it makes an ASS out of U and ME!

For example, you are waiting to pull out of a side junction and a van is indicating left to turn into your road. Do not assume that the driver will turn, allowing you to consider pulling out. All a flashing indicator tells you is that the bulb is working! There is also no guarantee that there is not a car or motorcyclist, out of sight, following close behind.

These examples of riding plans show how you can anticipate the actions of others. In conjunction with the five-point system which follows (page 20), riding plans form the basis of advanced motorcycling.

A riding plan in the country: the road may be very quiet, but anything can lie ahead; debris in the road would be spotted much later than the roof of a car.

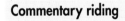

Commentary riding

The IAM has always recommended that car drivers should practise 'commentary driving', although this is no longer an obligatory part of the Advanced Driving Test. As an advanced motorcyclist, you can also benefit from trying this technique from time to time.

Commentary riding means describing out loud what you observe and what action you take. It gives you a very clear understanding of your anticipation of events and your response to them. You will almost certainly be amazed how much you can sharpen your observation and concentration. Fine-tuning your riding skills with commentary riding can also add interest to a dull trip.

Your state of mind

Self-control is an essential part of advanced riding. A powerful bike can out-distance most cars when traffic opens up, so why take risks?

Realising the importance of having a clear state of mind is one of the secrets of advanced motorcycling. The exhilaration and pleasure of riding are rightly savoured by motorcyclists, but these emotions should never come before self-control. Do not allow your enjoyment of riding along a quiet road on a bright spring morning, for example, to cause your speed to creep up unnoticed.

The aggression which some irresponsible riders show to other road users has no place in advanced motorcycling. Riding with self-control is not only the most satisfying way, but also the safest. On a high-performance machine you can out-distance most cars if you want to, so why take risks when you can go clear as soon as traffic and the road open up?

A timid approach can be just as dangerous as an aggressive one, for indecision can cause an accident in a situation demanding quick thinking. Good planning and observation, however, always gives you the measure of the situation around you, so occasions when you have to react to the unexpected in a split-second should be rare.

Every rider experiences occasions when special efforts in self-control and concentration have to be made. Aggressive, incompetent or reckless behaviour from drivers should never provoke you. Rise above it and keep yourself out of situations of 'road rage'. There are also times when it is important to recognise you are not at your best.

Extra concentration can be needed on a dull journey over familiar roads, or if you are tired after a bad night's sleep or a long day at work, or if you are distracted after a row at home. Being delayed by a traffic jam can make you agitated about arriving late. A cold or a mild dose of 'flu can slow your reactions, dull your judgement and make you bad-tempered. Riding under the influence of drugs or alcohol, needless to say, is out of the question.

Tolerance and courtesy

Take pride in being a tolerant and courteous rider at all times, especially at pedestrian crossings and in traffic. Even the most mild-mannered people become irritated, even angry, when other road users – particularly drivers who show little regard for the safety of motorcyclists – behave stupidly or inconsiderately.

Never let your riding be affected and remember that your behaviour may act as an example. Resist any temptation to retaliate. Stay calm, stay in control and stay alive.

If it is safe to give it, a 'thank you' wave to a considerate driver helps to encourage tolerance on the roads.

Your reaction time

Reaction times vary widely and are invariably longer than you think. A racing motorcyclist with naturally fast reactions and fired with adrenalin can react remarkably quickly, in as little as 0.2sec. The average rider is much slower to react: 0.4sec is excellent, 0.5sec is good and 0.8sec is satisfactory. Anything longer than a second is dangerously slow. If your reaction time is 0.5sec, at 70mph you travel 16 metres (nearly four car lengths) before you respond to a hazard.

To obtain a rough idea of your reaction time you could go to a driving centre equipped with a simulation tester. As an unscientific alternative you could play a party game: someone drops a pencil between your thumb and forefinger, and the speed with which you grip it shows how you compare with other people.

Your reactions slow down if you are tired, ill or under stress. Drugs, alcohol and even some prescribed medicines also dramatically impair your reactions. Keeping warm, with adequate clothing and frequent stops to restore circulation, helps to prevent your reactions slowing down in winter.

You can reduce the effect of your reaction time by reading the road ahead to observe when and where a hazard might occur. If you suspect danger, open your hand from the throttle grip and poise your fingers over the front brake lever. This will save a valuable split-second if you have to take action.

You must allow more reaction time at night because your eyes have to adjust constantly to changing levels of light. The pupil of the eye contracts quickly to adjust your vision when bright lights approach, but takes much longer to adapt to darkness again once the lights have gone.

There is a familiar claim from drivers or riders involved in an accident: 'I stopped dead'. Now that you know just how far you can travel while you are reacting to a hazard, you can see that this statement is ridiculous. No motorcycle can ever stop 'dead'. If it could, you certainly would not stop with it.

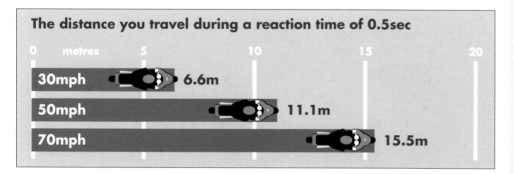

The distance you travel during a reaction time of 0.5sec

0 metres 5 10 15 20

30mph 6.6m
50mph 11.1m
70mph 15.5m

Other people's reactions

Always expect slow reactions from road users around you. Drivers can have slightly slower reactions because their feet and hands have further to move from accelerator to brake pedal, and from steering wheel to gear lever.

It is common for a rider involved in an accident with a car to complain that the driver 'had plenty of time to see me', and this might be right. But you cannot take for granted sharp reactions – or good observation – in another road user. An incident where a motorcyclist collides with a car because it pulls too slowly across his path could, in some circumstances, be blamed on both parties.

The planned system of riding

A procedure for all hazards

A systematic approach is needed whenever you change speed or course on your motorcycle. Scrutiny of accidents involving motorcycles shows that in most cases the rider makes an error at some point in the sequence, allowing inevitable consequences to take their course. Although the response may be wrong when an instant decision is required, very often the mistake which leads to an accident – perhaps the failure to glance in the mirror or reduce speed soon enough – occurs very early in the sequence.

Whether a hazard is a bend, a junction or just a parked vehicle, the five-point system of control (right) should be considered. This is a sequence of actions, although the first phase – Information – always overlaps the other four.

Remember that each of these features is to be considered, not slavishly put into action one after the other by rote. Spelled out in detail this may seem long-winded, but in practice it is simple, quick and necessary. The mnemonic 'IPSGA' makes it easy to remember. Practising it time and again will make it almost instinctive.

The system is not rigid: some situations call for extra checks in the mirrors before braking, while others require only parts of the procedure. By imposing this discipline on yourself and thinking well ahead, you will never be caught out by unexpected developments on the road ahead.

This planned method also minimises the danger of other road users being surprised by your actions. 'I didn't expect a right turn and it seemed safe to pass': this familiar excuse from car drivers can never be valid if you always make your intentions clear. As well as keeping other road users informed, it is important to check they have seen you and are reacting accordingly.

INFORMATION

Take information
Look all round, supplementing your use of mirrors with a shoulder check if necessary.

Use information
Using what you have observed, plan how to deal with the identified hazard.

Give information
Give a signal if it is helpful to other road users, using direction indicators, hand signalling, horn and flashed headlight as necessary.

POSITION
After giving a signal, take up the correct position on the road. You may need to repeat your rear observation.

SPEED
Adjust your speed to the correct level for the hazard by using the brakes or engine braking (or the throttle as necessary). You may need to repeat your rear observation.

GEAR
When you are travelling at the right speed, select the correct gear. Consider using the horn to warn others of your approach. Before any manoeuvre, consider a final check behind, using a lifesaver if necessary.

ACCELERATION
Once your motorcycle is on a straight course after the hazard, accelerate to a suitable speed.

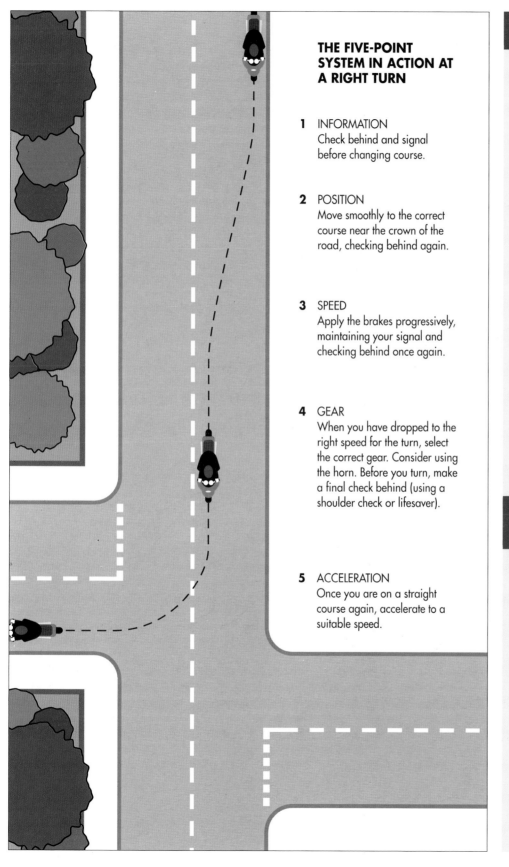

THE FIVE-POINT SYSTEM IN ACTION AT A RIGHT TURN

1 INFORMATION
Check behind and signal before changing course.

2 POSITION
Move smoothly to the correct course near the crown of the road, checking behind again.

3 SPEED
Apply the brakes progressively, maintaining your signal and checking behind once again.

4 GEAR
When you have dropped to the right speed for the turn, select the correct gear. Consider using the horn. Before you turn, make a final check behind (using a shoulder check or lifesaver).

5 ACCELERATION
Once you are on a straight course again, accelerate to a suitable speed.

Advanced checklist

- Absorb the five-point system of control: you apply it whenever you want to change speed or course, and it forms the basis for advanced riding.

- Remember there are two major reasons for using this method: you are always prepared for unexpected developments, and other road users are never surprised by your actions.

What the examiner looks for

- Do you have a good appreciation of the planned system of riding?

- Are signals given at the right time?

- Is your rear observation to a high standard?

- Are your actions made in sequence?

Observation

A basic skill of advanced riding

Good powers of observation, which demand practice, concentration and thought, keep you out of trouble. You need to absorb all the information around you and select from it what is useful.

All riders do this to a certain extent, but the advanced motorcyclist sees far more. Road sense is developed into an art, so that changing road and traffic conditions are constantly assessed, and the situation is read a long way ahead.

Forward observation

How much can you spot? A 4x4 is joining from the left, the car in front is braking, others are changing lanes without indicating, an illegally parked car may be about to move off (its brake lights are on), and there are red traffic lights in the distance.

been judged correctly? What if the driver pulls out anyway?

Remember, too, that many motorcycle accidents occur when no other vehicle is involved, and can fairly be attributed to poor forward observation by the rider. Was that bend more severe than it seemed? Was there diesel oil on the road? Maybe forward view was obstructed? Or perhaps speed was just excessive?

Some inexperienced riders look at the part of the road immediately in front of them, failing to notice sufficiently early the approach of junctions, roundabouts, changes in road surface, parked cars and any other potential hazards. You should concentrate your gaze on a point some way ahead, while at the same time taking in events even further in the distance as well as those closer to you and on either side.

When you start applying the five-point system (see pages 20-21) you will probably find all you can do is note mentally what you see ahead. After a while you should be able to say what you intend to do about the things you see. For example: 'That driver has children in the back seats and they are fighting, expect erratic course to be followed; maybe the car will pull over without signalling, so I will stay back until I can pass safely.'

One keen advanced rider, a doctor who specialises in race accident analysis, has coined the phrase, 'Remember, it's from eleven o'clock you get the shock!', meaning that most hazards loom from an angle to right or left. Forward observation must take account of the worst scenario. Maybe the driver in that side turning has impaired vision. Has my approach speed

This selective vision requires concentration and has to be developed with practice, so train yourself to cast an eye over as wide a field of vision as possible. Peripheral vision can take in a dog on the verge at the same time as you watch an overtaking car in the distance. Your centre of focus must be adjusted constantly according to speed and how far ahead the road is visible.

Vision

Make sure your vision is satisfactory. Research has shown that an alarming number of road users have eyesight deficiencies, yet most remain totally unaware that anything is wrong. Eyesight usually deteriorates so gradually that someone can have a vision defect and perhaps compensate for it subconsciously. People who try to avoid riding at night because they are not happy about their vision in darkness should acknowledge that it might also be less than perfect in daylight.

Eyesight problems affect safety. Having little or no sharp sight in one eye prevents good judgement of distance. Tunnel vision, the tendency to concentrate only on the view directly ahead, seriously restricts powers of observation; good peripheral sight is essential in order to see what is happening on either side of your bike. Long sight and short sight are extremely common (and proportionately worse at night), yet many riders remain unaware of it until eventually they are forced to have an eye test.

If you have not been to an optician for two years it would be wise to go for a check. If you need glasses make sure the frame you select fits comfortably inside your full-face helmet, or one-piece ski-type goggles if you wear an open-face helmet. If you already wear glasses, remember that it is an offence to ride without wearing them.

Your visor or goggles should be to BS4110, to be legal and to give reasonable resistance to scratching. If you prefer a graded-tint visor, remember that it can be used legally only in daylight. No sensible rider will lament the disappearance of the very dark visor, although there is still the anomaly of sunglasses being legal. You can combat problems of misting, especially if you wear glasses, by treating the surfaces of the visor with a trace of washing-up liquid or an anti-mist product.

Mirrors

It is important to be able to glance easily at the road behind without having to crook your head or twitch your shoulder out of the way. Inevitably there will be blind spots in your rearward vision, so adjust your mirrors to minimise these. Get to know the blind spots for your machine by checking them out on a quiet road.

Problems with vibration have largely disappeared, but some modern bikes have poorly positioned mirrors which do not give a clear view. Sometimes it is possible to move the mirrors outwards by packing out their mounting plates, or by cutting the stalks and extending them with short lengths of

tubing suitably threaded or welded in place. There are signs of sanity returning to the most recent models, but there is still a long way to go.

There are exceptions: the mirrors on Kawasaki GTR, BMW K100RT and Honda Gold Wing models are as near to being perfectly positioned as any rider could wish. Bar-end mirrors can be used on some machines, but many multi-cylinder models now have anti-vibration weights in their bar ends which should not be discarded.

Mirror position is important. The rider in the yellow tabard can see nothing immediately behind.

Rear observation

The three degrees of rear observation: from left, mirror check, shoulder check and lifesaver.

In the days when many motorcycles were not equipped with mirrors, or at best carried only one on the right handlebar, rear observation had to mean a physical look to the rear with your head turned. Most modern machines, however, have two well-placed mirrors and these can be used to good effect.

When the view is not clear or if you are uncertain about it, then nine times out of ten a shoulder check – a slight turn of the head which allows your peripheral vision to come into play – will suffice. Pulling away from rest is the classic example.

There tends to be confusion over the correct use of rear observation: some old hands say you should never look over your shoulder on the motorway, while at the other end of the spectrum primary instructors encourage pupils to look behind at virtually every lamp-post.

The classic 'lifesaver' glance behind still has its place, but can be reserved for major deviations when you do not have 100 per cent information on the traffic behind you. The fact that only five per cent of collisions involving a motorcycle occur from the rear must not allow

you to neglect the importance of knowing what is behind.

The essence of rear observation is based on flexibility. What am I looking for? What can be expected? Is it safe to take my eyes off the road ahead? All these questions need to be answered. Here are some helpful definitions:

- **Lifesaver** The classic roadcraft/police rider over-the-shoulder glance before turning right or left.
- **Shoulder check** A less pronounced rearward glance to check the offside or nearside blind spots, used to back up a mirror check when doubt exists.
- **Mirror check** Use of the mirrors for rearward observation; sometimes this will require a change of position to obtain a total rearward view.
- **Rear observation** The process of finding out what is behind you in the 180-degree arc from the handlebar ends rearwards.

Awareness of traffic behind is always necessary, especially when a vehicle is too close.

Poor surfaces

It is surprising how little effort average riders make to recognise road surface dangers in advance, complaining about slipperiness only after they have had a fright. You must always be ready for deterioration in the surface, looking ahead constantly for changes in its appearance.

Potholes and rippled surfaces can be found anywhere, even on quite major roads. Inadequate highway maintenance means that the quality of our roads generally seems to be deteriorating, and some parts of the country are worse than others. Keep an eye open at road works for loose gravel or wet tar, as both can be lethal. Passing traffic can spread gravel and chippings some distance from road works, so you may encounter a treacherous surface before you see any warning signs. Your first knowledge of it might come when you hear the sound of gravel being flicked up by your bike's tyres.

Besides the obvious dangers in rain, snow, ice or frost, the road can also be made slippery by mud, oil or dust. On the open road always watch for the mud – wet or dried – that can gather near a farm entrance or building site. Cobbles or wood-block surfaces in towns require special care, and even asphalt rubbed smooth by sheer weight of traffic demands respect, particularly in wet conditions.

Other wet weather hazards include cat's eyes, road studs, white lines, expansion joints in concrete roads, manhole covers, drains and sunken gullies. Battles with local authorities are still being waged about the pairs of surveying studs often placed on the rider's preferred line.

Worn areas in a surface need to be watched. The most common sign is where the coarse appearance of standard surface dressing is broken by polished areas where the top layer has been worn away. These patches require care: sometimes they can actually offer extra grip, but with fresh rain or morning dew they can become dangerous.

Look out for patches of diesel fuel spilled from overfilled lorry tanks. Once your bike's wheels are on this exceedingly slippery layer in a corner, you have virtually no chance of staying on if you are moving at speed. Apart from near a filling station, pools of oil can occur at any points – roundabouts, junctions, bends – where cornering forces cause fuel to spill from a full tank.

When a problem patch is spotted, use the five-point system to alter your course gradually, and as little as possible, to avoid it. There is no point in taking care to avoid a patch of ice under the shade of a hedge, or to miss some diesel on the road, only to stray into another danger.

Loose gravel is a common hazard, particularly at junctions and on bends.

Look out for subtle surface changes: sand may have been laid over spilled diesel fuel.

Selective observation

Good observation is essential to advanced riding, but the refinement of this skill comes in learning to be selective in what you observe. In a busy city centre, for example, you need to distinguish what should be acted upon and what can be ignored. Some pointers will give you an idea of the range of visual information which helps you to become a safer rider.

At first glance there seems to be no-one about in this street, but notice those feet beneath the parked van.

• Unexpected movements by parked vehicles must always be allowed for, especially if you can see a driver inside. The vehicle can suddenly move into your path if the driver sets off without thinking, or someone might open a door.
• Telegraph poles changing course can give early warning of a corner, but remember that occasionally the wires can track straight on while the road bends.

Telegraph wires can indicate the course of a bend before you actually see it.

• Crosswinds can blow through gaps between buildings, hills or trees and buffet your machine off its course.
• Give stationary vans a wide berth, especially on quiet roads, in case the driver gets out unexpectedly.
• Be especially alert with pedestrians in wet weather: people who are hurrying for shelter or keeping their heads down against the rain are not always so careful.

• Always give cyclists plenty of room. As a motorcyclist, you should be sensitive to their problems. Not all cyclists are skilled on their machines, so always expect a wobble. A cyclist might also steer round a pothole or drain just as you are coming up to pass.
• Intelligent observation of parked vehicles can give you early warning. A car with its reversing lights on is about to move backwards. A puff of smoke or merely a vibration ·from the exhaust means that the driver has just started the engine and may pull into your path.
• If you are behind a bus, a passenger putting a hand up to the bell suggests the bus is about to stop.
• A cloud of smoke from the exhaust of a lorry climbing a hill tells you that its driver has changed down and will be travelling even more slowly. If you are riding down a hill, a slow-moving lorry coming towards you could conceal a car whose driver is about to attempt a rash overtaking manoeuvre.
• Is the driver of the car ahead of you paying full attention? Someone using a mobile 'phone, turning round to tell off children in the back seat or having an animated conversation with a passenger is not concentrating on the job in hand.

• Any parked vehicle can hide a pedestrian about to step out, so look for tell-tale feet visible beneath it. School buses, ice cream vans and delivery vans need particular care.
• Any pedestrians should be observed carefully. A child can dash into the road without looking; an old person, perhaps with failing eyesight or hearing, might not see you coming; a dog off a lead could do anything.

• Reflections in a shop window at an urban junction or corner can show you an approaching vehicle before you actually see it.
• Give more room to the aggressive or sloppy driver: drop further back from a driver ahead trying to overtake when there is no realistic opportunity, or someone who is paying more attention to finding a particular address in town than to the surrounding traffic.

Reflections in windows can provide helpful information at junctions and corners in town.

Stationary vehicles: a special warning

This Post Office van presents two potential problems. Apart from blocking the view down the road, it could move away without warning.

The advanced rider must pay special attention to stationary and slow-moving cars, particularly at junctions. One research study into the causes of accidents involving motorcycles has revealed that 68 per cent of those resulting in injury occurred at junctions. Of these, 73 per cent happened when the motorcycle was travelling straight ahead and a car was starting its manoeuvre.

Car drivers who fail to see an approaching motorcyclist, or who misjudge its speed, are one of the most frequent and dangerous hazards you face on your machine. Careful observation picks up potential danger well in advance.

Road signs

Anyone who has passed the government test should know all road signs, but it is still worth referring to the *Highway Code* periodically to check that you remember all the warning signs (triangular), advisory signs (rectangular) and mandatory signs (circular).

British roads are quite well provided with signs, and all of them are erected by local authorities for a purpose; you should know at a glance what any sign is telling you. Do not fall into the habit of ignoring signs except when you are searching for particular information, for all of them help in the process of thinking ahead.

Road signs always provide valuable information. Two signs on one pole should be read from the top: here a bend to the left is followed by a junction to the right.

Advanced checklist

- Observation depends upon good eyesight, so make sure you have had your eyes tested recently, even if you are confident that your vision has not deteriorated.

- Concentrate your gaze on a point some way ahead, while at the same time taking in events even further in the distance, closer to you and on either side.

- Use your mirrors regularly, but remember that there are many occasions – such as pulling away from rest, turning at junctions or overtaking – when a shoulder check or lifesaver is needed.

- Always be watchful for changes in the road surface which could reduce the grip of your bike's tyres.

- Develop the skills of selective observation so that you have an eye for any situation which might require action from you.

What the examiner looks for

- Do you read the road ahead properly and show that you have a good sense of anticipation?

- Do you demonstrate the ability to judge speed and distance?

- Do you react early enough to hazards?

- Do you use the mirror frequently and intelligently?

- Are shoulder checks and lifesavers used when appropriate?

- Do you keep an eye on the road surface, especially in bad weather?

- Are signals, signs and road markings observed, obeyed and approached correctly?

2 ADVANCED MOTORCYCLE CONTROL

Braking

Use of front and rear brakes

If you practise, as an aspiring advanced rider you will come to understand the finer points of using the front and rear brakes. Braking always causes the combined weight of rider and machine to be thrown forward so that the front tyre is forced

Weight transfer makes the rear wheel more likely to lock under heavy braking, particularly on a poor surface.

more strongly against the road.

On a dry and even surface this weight transfer usually increases the front tyre's grip and makes the front brake more effective, but on a wet or poor surface it significantly increases the chances of a front-wheel skid. At the same time, the corresponding reduction in weight on the rear wheel makes this more likely to lock up too.

A locked wheel is not only completely useless as a brake, but it also removes the rider's control until pressure on the brake is released to get the wheel turning again. A machine with anti-lock brakes, of course, does this for you (see page 30).

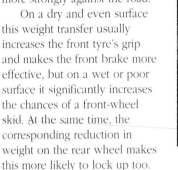

Another braking aid is available when surfaces are treacherous – the braking effect of the engine when the throttle is closed. In fact the truly skilled rider uses anticipation and good judgement of speed to carry out most retardation on engine braking alone.

The front tyre is loaded more strongly under hard braking, adding to grip on a good surface but increasing the chance of a skid on a poor one.

Slippery surfaces

On a dry road the advanced rider puts around 75 per cent of the braking effort to the front wheel and around 25 per cent to the rear wheel, but this distribution must be adjusted when conditions are not perfect.

When a good surface is wet about 50 per cent should go to each wheel, but in worse conditions – such as when a surface is loose or icy, or affected by wet leaves, mud or oil – the rear brake only should be used, taking care to avoid

locking the wheel. On such surfaces the front brake can lock very easily.

If you do lock either wheel when braking, you need to release the pressure momentarily to allow the locked wheel to turn again, and then reapply the brake more gently. Maximum braking effort is achieved at the point just before a wheel locks.

Select a good patch of road for braking whenever possible, and allow a margin for road surface changes when judging

your braking. If you spot a shiny section of asphalt leading into a bend, plan your braking so that your speed is reduced before you reach it. Ease off the pressure momentarily if you find the surface deteriorating under your wheels.

A surprising number of riders seem to press on regardless of road surface, only to find that they need to resort to wild body contortions just to stay upright when the bike starts to slide.

Smooth braking

If you apply the skills of advanced riding you should seldom have to brake fiercely. Your braking will be smooth and progressive, and you will leave that extra margin in case you need it.

When braking to a stop, use engine retardation for the initial phase then progressively apply the brakes for two-thirds to three-quarters of the available distance. If you ease off the brakes as speed comes down you will minimise the front fork dip that is the mark of the novice.

Using the lower gears for added engine retardation in conjunction with gentle braking can help on steep downhill stretches or when the surface is slippery.

Braking distance

Many riders leave a distance which is adequate only if the vehicle in front slows down at a normal rate, but just occasionally it stops a good deal quicker if it hits another vehicle ahead. The safe distance is one in which you can come to a complete stop in an emergency.

The safe distance is the sum of braking and thinking distance. While it is true that you should be able to react more quickly in an emergency than a car driver because your hand and foot can be poised over the controls, you must allow for reaction time (see page 19) – the time it takes the brain to assess the situation and send the 'apply brakes' message. Someone who can do this in under 0.5sec has superb reactions, yet in this time a motorcycle travelling at 70mph covers 16 metres (nearly four car lengths) before the brakes go on, and if your brakes and tyres are 100 per cent then you will only come to rest in another 75 metres.

It follows that you need to leave enough distance when following other vehicles to stop safely.

Make sure you know the exact braking distances for various speeds, but in practice the advanced rider judges safety by using roadcraft rather than calling up figures from memory.

Good judgement of braking distance applies in all riding, whether following other vehicles or braking progressively on the approach to hazards such as junctions.

Braking on bends

Perceived wisdom used to state that braking on bends was absolutely taboo, and an old story about a police student on an advanced course is worth repeating. Having survived an excursion through a hedge that resulted from over-enthusiastic cornering, our student crawls back to the roadside grinning sheepishly. 'Well, I didn't brake, Sarge!' he says to his instructor.

Of course it is advisable to brake when your machine is upright and travelling in a straight line, varying the pressure and front/rear distribution according to road conditions. But just occasionally you might find you are faced with an emergency leaving you no choice but to brake unexpectedly during the course of a bend. In those split seconds, which can seem such a long time, try to remember three things.

• Concentrate on where you want to go. It is surprising how many riders look at the peripheral danger spots instead of aiming out of trouble.

• If you can, sit the bike up and brake hard, releasing the brakes if you must lean again to avoid the main danger.

• If all else fails, decide how you are going to lay down the machine. Even fairly solid objects, or better still a hedge, are preferable to opposing vehicles.

Reading this advice takes far longer than putting it into practice, but plant it in your mind in case you ever need it.

Anti-lock braking

The latest disc designs offer superb braking under all conditions. In fact, on some superbikes the front brakes are bordering on the over-sensitive, making it possible to lock up the front wheel on a dry road with only light finger pressure. The skilled rider can use the tremendous power which these brakes offer, but for most levels of competence something else is needed.

That 'something else' – anti-lock braking or ABS – is now commonly available to the car driver, and motorcycle manufacturers are following the same route. From the first days of anti-lock car brakes, experiments began with similar brakes for two-wheelers although early mechanical designs were cumbersome. They gave an unacceptable penalty in unsprung weight, and a lot of development was needed before they could be mass-produced.

The advent of on-board computers and microchip technology on the automotive scene, however, meant that electronic controls could be used, and BMW's ABS was the first in the world to be offered for motorcycles. Yamaha, among others, now offer an ABS system too, and Honda's ABS/TCS version has the added refinement of traction control, a device which limits the power output as soon as the rear wheel starts to spin.

Those who have experienced ABS-equipped motorcycles cannot fail to be impressed by their uncanny stability under braking on a slippery surface, but the systems add significantly to the purchase price of all the marques that offer them.

Even without anti-lock, modern motorcycle brakes are superb: paired front discs on a Honda Fireblade (below) and a cable-operated rear drum on a BMW R100GS (below right).

Familiarity with your machine

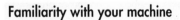

Considerable skill is required to brake effectively under adverse conditions. You are strongly advised to discover the braking ability of your machine, perhaps in a private car park or on a quiet road, before you need to use it in earnest.

It is a sad fact that many motorcyclists, and car drivers for that matter, have come to grief because they did not use all the braking power and distance that was available in the fractions of seconds before they hit something. Find out your bike's potential under your choice of conditions rather than in a situation not under your control. Choose a good surface and try really hard, braking from 30mph, first with front brake, then with rear brake and then with both. You will be amazed how short a distance you need to come to rest.

It is good practice to give the brakes a dab when starting any journey to make sure they are working well. A quick visual check before every trip is also wise, as you may spot frayed cable ends, worn cable casings or leaks from hydraulic pipes.

Gearchanging

Using the gearbox

The advanced rider will always be travelling in the right gear. Using the gearbox correctly is not only essential to good riding but it also reduces mechanical wear and tear.

Good use of the gearbox has to be developed with experience, to the point where you have an almost instinctive knack, coupled with use of the rev counter, for knowing which gear will produce the best response.

The trend of some of the sophisticated designs from Japanese manufacturers is towards more high-revving engines (some capable of more than 10,000rpm) with narrow power bands which require five-speed or even six-speed gearboxes. On a machine such as this, with little throttle response outside its tight power band,

In addition to your mechanical sensitivity, use the rev counter to decide when to change gear.

correct gear selection becomes even more important.

Even experienced riders can be guilty of common faults: staying in top gear for too long so that a down-change is forced by the engine starting to labour; moving away in second gear and slipping the clutch; and running up and down the gears so excessively that the engine spends much of its time revving hard and wearing itself out.

You should keep the engine within its comfortable range so that it is neither labouring nor racing too fast, and prepare for any hazard by selecting a lower gear – for better acceleration or braking – well in advance.

Slowing down

As you change down, you should use sufficient throttle in neutral to bring the revs up to the right level for the lower gear, so that it engages as smoothly as possible when you release the clutch. Smooth clutch action and a balanced throttle are especially important in slippery conditions, since closing the throttle and releasing the clutch sharply can cause the rear wheel to skid.

Intelligent use of the gearbox's braking effect is an integral part of motorcycling. Using the gears to slow down your machine is particularly valuable on wet and slippery

surfaces as the engine, on closed throttle, gives a gentle braking effect which is less likely to lock the rear wheel than using the brake alone.

On a good surface a blend of engine braking and brakes is used for gradual slowing down, but the engine can play a greater part the worse the conditions get, so that on ice or loose gravel the brake can be ignored except for coming to a final halt.

Using neutral

Select neutral only when virtually at a standstill. Always do it when at rest for any appreciable time, to avoid wearing out the clutch components and actuating mechanism by running the engine with first gear engaged while waiting to move off again. Inexperienced motorcyclists tend to hold the clutch lever in the withdrawn position for

long periods while waiting to move off.

Some riders develop the bad habit of selecting neutral some time before they stop, perhaps when approaching traffic lights or a junction, and coasting over the final distance.

Acceleration and speed

Using power wisely

If you ride a high-performance machine you will know all about the self-control you must apply in using its capabilities safely on the road. But ask yourself a question: do you always use power wisely or are there occasions when restraint deserts you? The advanced motorcyclist enjoys using the acceleration of a powerful machine, but only when it is safe and appropriate, and when it will not surprise or

inconvenience other road users.

Although the upper reaches of a superbike's performance cannot be used legally on public roads, it is natural to be curious about what your machine can do. Why not satisfy your curiosity by taking your bike to one of the organised track days that take place at some racing circuits? Assuming you respond properly to the expert tuition that will precede a track outing,

Confine your use of strong acceleration to situations, such as overtaking, when it is safe and useful.

you can ride fast legally and in relative safety. Self-control should come that much more easily after this experience.

Acceleration sense

Fine-tuning your acceleration sense adds precision to your riding. When closing on slower traffic, come off the throttle at the right moment so you ease towards the safe following distance without using the brakes.

Riding for pleasure along a quiet B-road, letting the revs climb between corners, is the best way to appreciate your machine's performance and learn exactly how it responds to throttle openings in each gear.

You can perfect your control of your machine by developing an instinctive feeling for the engine's torque and power characteristics, and for the changes in stability that occur as you use varying degrees of acceleration.

Time throttle, gearchange and clutch actions accurately to avoid unsettling your bike. Snatched gearchanges and on-

off use of the throttle may get you up the road a whisker more quickly, but your bike will dive and squat with each change and the rear tyre will fight for grip every time you apply power. You should use acceleration in a controlled way: unwind the throttle gradually, not suddenly, before you change gear, and go back on the power with the same progression.

Fine-tuning your acceleration sense adds interest and pleasure to any journey, and leads to much less use of the brakes. On a twisty country road, judge the precise point to stop accelerating after a bend so that engine braking alone brings you down to the right speed for the next corner. Do the same when closing in on a slower vehicle: come off the throttle at the point that allows your bike to ease neatly towards the safe following distance without using the brakes. Use this technique when you see a speed limit sign in the distance, so that you drop to the exact speed the moment you pass the sign. Refining your

acceleration sense in these ways can give you great pride in your riding.

There are many occasions, such as overtaking or blending with traffic from a slip road, when strong acceleration is required. If a slower vehicle on a dual-carriageway starts to move into your lane just as you are passing it, accelerating out of trouble may be better than braking. It is just as important, though, to recognise the circumstances when acceleration should be used with restraint.

Use the gears correctly so that strong acceleration is always available if you need it. Some riders of large-capacity touring machines hang on to the higher gears and rely too much on the engine's low-down torque, denying themselves the opportunity in an emergency to use the stronger acceleration available in lower gears.

When you see a speed limit in the distance, aim to drop to the exact speed the moment you pass the sign, preferably using only engine braking.

Speed limits

Some roads allow you legally to travel at speeds which frankly are not safe, so you should use good judgement whenever you are riding. Main roads in rural areas sometimes permit you to pass through a straggle of houses at 60mph, a speed which would prevent you coping with a child or a dog running out of a concealed driveway. On a busy high street it might be reckless to ride at more than 15mph, even though double this speed is legal.

Riding too slowly can be dangerous if you hold up traffic, inviting frustrated drivers to pass you, sometimes without giving you enough room. On congested roads you can face a difficult judgement if strict observance of a speed limit means you travel more slowly than the general flow. In such circumstances safety and common-sense dictate that you blend into your surroundings, but speed limits should be obeyed and any breach of the law during your Advanced Motorcycling Test will result in failure.

The discipline you need for the Advanced Motorcycling Test should be applied to all your riding, even if you think there are occasions when a higher speed is safe. It may be tempting to wind your speed a little higher than 60mph on an open stretch of road with wide verges, excellent visibility, no traffic and no side turnings, but remember that you cannot enjoy advanced motorcycling if you do not have a licence.

A basic rule of advanced motorcycling is that you should ride at a speed which allows you to stop within the distance you can see. Follow this principle rather than treat a speed limit at face value.

Speed limits should not be taken at face value. Passing an isolated house or concealed driveway at 60mph on a country road may be legal, but not necessarily safe.

Warming the engine

Mechanical sympathy means that you should avoid using strong acceleration until your bike's engine and gearbox have warmed up, unless you need to take emergency action. Taking your machine to 10,000rpm before the oil is warm will significantly shorten the life of the engine, and there is a case for saying that you, the rider, also need to get into the swing of things before easing your speed higher.

Modern engines with fuel injection tend not to suffer flat-spots and hesitancy even when cold, but a bike with a carburettor might give unreliable acceleration while it is warming up. Remember this when pulling away from junctions in your first few miles on a cold morning, and avoid overtaking until you are certain the engine is performing cleanly.

Advanced checklist

- On a high-performance machine use acceleration with restraint when other road users are around you.

- Accelerate decisively when it is appropriate, such as when overtaking or joining traffic from a slip road.

- Develop acceleration sense so that you ease on and off the power at the right moment and avoid unnecessary braking.

- Obey speed limits, but think about the times when riding at the limit is too fast.

What the examiner looks for

- Do you accelerate smoothly and progressively?

- Is your use of acceleration excessive or insufficient for the road, traffic and weather conditions?

- Do you use acceleration at the right time and place?

- Bearing in mind the road, traffic and weather conditions, do you keep up a reasonable pace and maintain good progress?

- Are you careful not to obstruct other vehicles by riding too slowly?

- Are speed limits observed?

Sympathy and understanding

Mechanical sympathy

Even if you do not consider yourself technically minded, a basic understanding of how a motorcycle works will add to your pleasure in owning and riding your machine. It is beyond the purpose of this book to embark on a detailed description of motorcycle engineering, but try to learn more if you feel mechanically ignorant. Obtain a good specialist manual for your machine if you want to extend your knowledge beyond the owner's handbook.

Advanced riding techniques go hand in hand with mechanical sympathy. Helped by knowledge of the machine and respect for it, the advanced rider avoids clumsy or violent use of the controls, thereby minimising wear and tear on all mechanical parts. When conditions are right the machine's ability is used to the full, but never abused.

'Grand Prix' starts at traffic lights are exciting but very anti-social as well as dangerous, as is the dubious fashion for 'wheelies' among those who try to emulate race stars. As well as giving motorcycling a bad image, these flamboyant manoeuvres increase tyre wear, use more fuel and give the transmission chain and sprockets a hard time. Late braking shortens the life of pads or shoes and wears out tyres more quickly.

Rear chain oilers extend chain life greatly and reduce the frequency of adjustment. Whether or not a chain oiler is fitted, do keep the chain correctly adjusted. If it is too tight, it will ruin the output shaft bearings in the gearbox. If too loose, it may jump the rear sprocket and lock the back wheel. When a bike passes you, glance at its chain. After a few days' observation you will see ample evidence of neglect.

After the chain the clutch is the most abused part of a motorcycle's transmission. Common faults which quickly ruin a clutch are slipping it to avoid changing gear, dropping it in suddenly with the engine at high revs, using it to hold the bike stationary on a hill, and disengaging it for long periods instead of selecting neutral when stopped.

This last fault is the mark of the novice or careless rider. Admittedly some clutches are prone to drag and make neutral selection not exactly easy, but as you get to know your machine you will become practised in clutch and gear pedal control for traffic light stops and other lengthy hold-ups.

The engine can be abused as well. By all means enjoy its performance when it is safe to do so, but letting the revs soar habitually to the red line will wear it out more quickly. Likewise you can labour an engine by asking it to pull hard at low revs in a high gear.

Looking after your tyres

Check tyre pressures once a week even if your tyres appear to hold their pressure well over a long period. Since the pressure gauges on garage air lines are often inaccurate, use a small pocket gauge. Always carry out your check at the start of a journey when the air in the tyres is cold.

Follow the manufacturer's recommended pressures, using common sense to make slight variations – adding a few pounds to the rear tyre when carrying a passenger for instance – if you feel they are necessary. At the same time prise any small stones out of the treads and check the sidewalls for cuts or bulges.

Under-inflation causes serious problems when cornering because the sidewalls can move sideways relative to the wheel rim when the bike is leaned over. This gives a disconcerting squirming sensation or even a dangerous wobble, and straight-line stability may suffer too. Under-inflation also causes heat to build up in a tyre, increasing the rate of wear and leading in extreme circumstances to chunks of tread breaking off the tyre carcass. Soft tyres are more easily damaged and increase fuel consumption.

Over-inflation can occur if an inaccurate pressure gauge is used, and results in the tyre bulging in the centre of the tread pattern so that only a small section is in contact with the road. As much as half of the tyre's grip can be lost, and the central part of the tread will wear rapidly.

The law requires that a tyre must be replaced when tread depth over three-quarters of its width has worn down to 1mm (the figure is 1.6mm for car tyres). This is remarkably lenient. A tyre's grip in the wet will have deteriorated considerably by this point, so it is wise to consider replacement when the tread depth is around 3mm. Riding with badly worn treads also increases the possibility of a puncture.

Tyre technicalities

For many years it was said that the benefits of radial tyres enjoyed by drivers could not be shared by motorcyclists. However, tyre designers have been able to meet this challenge and nowadays semi-radial and fully-radial motorcycle tyres are available.

Most radial motorcycle tyres are tubeless, are designed for

Check pressures when tyres are cold, using your own gauge for consistency (above). A selection of badly worn tyres, all beyond the margins of safety (above right).

wide rims and have a low aspect ratio (the ratio of height to width of the tyre's cross-section). They will not fit on rims narrower than those for which they are designed, and any attempt to use a wider tubeless tyre on an unsuitable rim will run the risk of inducing tyre creep and instability. At worst, the tyre can even come off the rim when subjected to strong forces.

Provided this advice is followed, there will be very noticeable benefits if your machine will accept radial tyres. Your bike will run more true, it will be less susceptible to 'white-lining', cornering power will be increased, braking ability improved and there should be at least 20 per cent more mileage compared with the wear rate of a cross-ply.

Whatever type of tyre you choose, it is essential to follow the manufacturer's instructions on tread, size, profile and type. Many tyres are not

interchangeable between front and rear wheels, and often the replacement tread will be different from the original. A word about tyre designations may also be useful.

Two examples from opposite ends of the speed range are 110/90-18 S and 170/60-17 ZR. The first is a tyre of 110mm width and a section height of 90 per cent of the width, fits an 18in rim and is rated for speeds up to 113mph, as used on the rear wheel of light to middleweight machines. The 170mm tyre

has a height only 60 per cent of the width (a low-profile design), and it fits a 17in rim. Z shows it is good for speeds over 150mph, and R that it is of radial construction. Between these extremes are H-rated tyres for speeds up to 130mph and V-rated for 130-150mph. V and Z obviously come into race specifications.

The best advice is to stick with the speed rating of your bike's original tyres: they will suit the performance, even if the top speed capability is academic. It is plainly a waste of money to pay for tyres which are designed to go faster than your motorcycle can.

As for choosing between different brands, it is impossible to give definite guidance. Take advice from tyre specialists and other owners on how different tyres suit your particular machine, and if possible borrow a bike to try out; it has been known for tyres on the same bike to suit one rider's style and not another's.

Wet-weather performance is the most important consideration: a tyre which copes well with wet surfaces should be fine in the dry, and it is in wet weather that you really need to be riding on the best possible tyres. Once you are sure of this factor, consider also durability, ride quality and cost.

3 APPLYING ADVANCED MOTORCYCLING METHODS

Positioning

Exceptions to the 'keep left' rule

Keeping well out from parked cars gives you a better view of approaching hazards, as well as removing the danger of someone opening a door in your path.

Although the basic rule of the road is that you must keep left except when turning right or overtaking, there are many occasions when a motorcyclist need not keep to the normal position, which is between one and two metres from the nearside. If you slavishly follow the letter of the law, you will often find yourself facing the same difficulties which any driver of a left-hand drive car encounters in Britain – a poor field of vision.

When it is safe to do so, you should take up a position which gives the best view of the road and traffic ahead. Provided no other vehicles are close behind, this means moving towards the crown of the road, such as when approaching an intersection or a junction on the left. This temporary position gives you an earlier view of vehicles approaching on the adjoining road, since your field of vision across the junction is broader. Any driver waiting to pull out from the side road also has an earlier view of you in this position.

When approaching junctions with 'stop' signs, traffic lights, filter lights or lanes marked for taking a left or right turn, you should take up a position in the centre of the appropriate lane well in advance. Not only does this help motorists to notice you, but it also means that they are less likely to force you out of the lane by pulling close alongside. Even if your lane dictates your path through the junction, it is still best to signal in order to reinforce your intentions.

A motorcycle which appears to be ridden confidently, well into the road, is more noticeable and seems more important, discouraging drivers from pulling out into the rider's path. A driver is more likely to think there is time to nip out ahead of an approaching motorcycle if it appears to be ridden timidly and close to the kerb.

There are many other situations where a position nearer the centre of the road is preferable. Keeping well out when passing parked vehicles gives a better view of approaching hazards such as pedestrian crossings; it allows you to avoid the drains, manhole covers, puddles and loose gravel which can disrupt the road surface near the kerb; and it gives you greater control and vision through bends (see page 39). Of course, you must always be careful to check behind you when riding nearer to the centre of the road and be sure that oncoming drivers can see you from a good distance.

Remember that over-indulgence in positioning can look very odd to any untutored driver behind you. So, when being followed, modify the extent of your positioning commensurate with gaining a good forward view, reducing speed if necessary. Always sacrifice position for safety when faced with oncoming traffic.

Positioning with other vehicles

It is important to understand the value of good position in relation to other vehicles travelling in your direction. You must never ride too close to a vehicle in front for the obvious reason that you need to be able to stop in the distance available, but it is less widely realised that keeping a good distance gives much better visibility.

When riding behind a lorry, for example, the best view ahead is available if you hold station even further back than the safe stopping distance. Keeping well back gives earlier warning of junctions on the nearside, parked cars, oncoming traffic, pedestrian crossings, traffic

slowing down ahead of you, and bad patches of road.

If the driver behind is not too close, you can broaden your view by moving gently from nearside to offside in your carriageway so that you can see round the vehicle ahead on both sides. At the right distance behind this can be done with relatively little change of course.

Good position behind a lorry (right). Poor position – too close and too far to the left – closes down the view of the road ahead (far right).

Positioning on the open road

Good position through a left-hand bend (above). Poor position – too close to the nearside – again closes down the view of the road ahead (right).

The advanced rider really stands out from the novice in the ability to select the best position when following other vehicles through bends (see also page 39).

The ideal line for a right-hand bend is the one which an advanced rider would take if the road were empty. You should keep to the left on approach for a wider view through the bend, move towards the centre line through the bend to 'straighten' it (after checking your mirror and without crossing the line) and then edge back to the left for the earliest view up the straight stretch which follows. Straightening the bend in this way gives a safer, shallower arc through the turn, leaving you in a good

position if there is an opportunity to overtake.

Right-hand bends can present better opportunities for overtaking because the road ahead becomes visible sooner. But at the apex never move so close to the centre line that oncoming drivers are alarmed or you put yourself at risk. Always make sure no vehicles are close behind before altering your position on the road.

Left-hand bends should also be taken on a line that maximises your view ahead. This means moving towards the centre line on the approach so you can see further into the bend, and holding this course until the view opens up. When you see the straight stretch ahead, easing back to the left allows you to straighten the last part of the bend and begin your acceleration earlier.

Cornering

Control through bends

Safe cornering on open roads is one of the great pleasures of motorcycling.

Modern tyres in good condition allow a rider to make excellent progress through bends, and therein lies much of the appeal of motorcycling for the enthusiast. The challenge of dealing with a series of curves on country roads can be very enjoyable. But you should always remember that the contact areas of motorcycle tyres are very small compared with those on the average car.

The golden rule is always to ride at a speed commensurate with your forward view. If you enter a bend at an excessive speed which does not give you time to react to any change in traffic conditions or road surface, you may be faced with emergency braking when the bike is banked over too far to recover.

You must be aware of the braking and handling characteristics of your machine if you intend to explore higher cornering speeds. Some models tend to sit up under firm braking, while others will become less stable if the throttle is closed in mid-bend or if gear changes are handled roughly.

If the road surface is good, you will find that moderate acceleration as you progress through the bend will increase the weight on the rear wheel and give a feeling of stability.

Camber influences the way you tackle a bend. Camber assists you on a left-hander and a fair amount of banking is achievable, but it acts against you on a right-hander.

Modern roads have a 'super-elevated' profile. Super-elevation banks up the whole width of the road towards the outside edge of the bend, making the slope favourable in both directions.

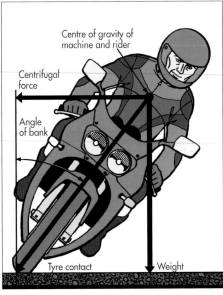

Centre of gravity of machine and rider

Centrifugal force

Angle of bank

Tyre contact

Weight

The forces which act on a motorcycle when it is banked through a corner.

Cornering at higher speeds

It is fashionable for sports machine riders to try to emulate their race circuit heroes by climbing all over their bikes, and getting the knee-scraper pads on their leathers nicely scuffed. When you consider the reserves of adhesion offered by modern tyres you realise that for all legal speeds this behaviour might be fun but it is not necessary.

This is not to say that track experience is a waste of time. Special track days are organised on several UK circuits, and if you want to find out a bit more about your

machine's handling and a lot more about your courage they are worth the money. The most famous course is run on the Nürburgring in Germany, and instructors there will explain the effects of heavy braking, cornering and counter-steering to aspiring high-performance riders.

Counter-steering takes place automatically when a machine is banked over, because the bars have to be turned away from the direction of travel to initiate the turn. Conscious application of counter-steering can be of vital use in extreme cornering conditions, so it is useful to find out what really happens when you take a bend reasonably quickly.

Positioning on bends

Positioning to maximise the view on a left-hander (right) and a right-hander (far right).

Considerations of safety, road surface, other road users and visibility all affect your decision about how much of the width of your carriageway you use when negotiating a bend, since the best course means optimising your position on the road. However, you can use the techniques which follow surprisingly often.

For left-hand bends you obtain the best view around the corner by taking up a position towards the centre of the road, after checking your mirrors and adjusting your speed. You should hold this position through the bend until the view opens up, then

How your view can be improved with good positioning. From a line towards the crown of the road, this oncoming car appears slightly earlier.

sweep smoothly in towards the nearside to straighten the last part of the corner. Flattening the curve once you have a good view brings your machine upright slightly earlier and allows you to accelerate more strongly out of the corner.

You should always be certain it is safe to take this preferred course. If you are in any doubt you should hold the nearside all the way through. Riding in dense traffic, approaching roadworks, taking account of a poor road surface or seeing skid marks on the road are all occasions when you should slow down and keep firmly to the nearside until you have a clear view forwards.

Maximising your view on right-hand bends means that you approach on the nearside and then choose a gradual curve towards the centre as soon as you can see through the corner. This point will occur sooner on an open bend than on one bounded by tall hedges or walls.

As well as improving your view, this more gradual course gives your bike's tyres better grip since they do not have to cope with so much adverse camber at the apex of the bend. You can accelerate slightly after you pass the apex to help your bike back to a nearside course.

Emergency action

You must remember two facts about your machine's behaviour when faced with an emergency, such as someone else having an accident in front of you on a bend. Acceleration will tend to push the bike wide, while lifting off or braking will tend to

tighten its line. Doing either in excess will cause a skid and possibly make you have an accident too.

In an extreme situation sit the bike up and brake hard to reduce speed, even if you have to lean it over again to stay on course.

Advanced checklist

- Corners are best taken smoothly at a constant speed or with moderate acceleration once the exit line is visible.

- You must avoid excessive braking or acceleration on bends unless an emergency leaves you no alternative.

- When road and traffic conditions permit, place your machine for the best view through a corner, using the positioning described for left- and right-handers.

- Always sacrifice position for safety in an emergency.

What the examiner looks for

- Are bends and corners taken safely and fluidly?

- Do you position your machine properly to improve your view?

- Is speed through corners judged well?

- Do you ride with the general cornering fluency that really marks out the advanced motorcyclist?

Overtaking

The motorcyclist's advantage

Never overtake approaching a junction. Right turns are especially dangerous: the vehicle you are passing could turn right without signalling, or a driver could emerge from the junction into your path.

One of the great benefits of motorcycling is that you can make quicker journeys than other traffic over congested roads. In the right circumstances you can pass long rows of slow-moving vehicles on busy trunk roads, or move quietly to the front of any queue at traffic lights and junctions. If the road is wide enough, it is even possible to overtake when there is a solid white line because you do not need to cross it. All these things allow you to make better progress than a car driver in the UK.

Judging when to overtake

You need to develop good judgement of speed, distance and your machine's acceleration. When assessing whether there is time to overtake safely, take into account the huge difference between overtaking and closing speeds. Overtaking a car moving at 45mph when you are doing 60mph means you will pass it at a cyclist's pace, but the approaching lorry in the distance may also be doing 60mph. You will close with the lorry at 120mph, or 55 metres per second.

You should never overtake when approaching a side turning. Junctions to the right are particularly dangerous: the vehicle you plan to overtake could turn right without warning, or a vehicle could emerge from the junction. One scenario happens all too often: a driver pauses to join a main road, looks to the right to check that nothing is coming, and then pulls out without considering that an overtaking car or motorcycle could be approaching from the left.

As well as signposted junctions, small lanes, driveways and laybys should be treated with suspicion. The white lines bordering the road are particularly helpful to an observant rider. A section of broken lines interrupting a solid line warn of a minor turning, often well before you actually see it.

There is a simple guiding rule: if in doubt hold back.

How to overtake safely

When waiting for an overtaking opportunity, make sure you have a good view by taking up a position near the centre of the road and hanging far enough back so that you can see well past the vehicle ahead. You must be certain no hazards are approaching and a suitable gap lies ahead for you to pull in again safely. Just occasionally a large lorry can follow other traffic so closely that you could embark on an overtaking move only to find that you have to pass two or three vehicles in one manoeuvre.

The skill of safe overtaking lies in the build-up: from here it is a case of firm acceleration.

When an opportunity looks imminent, check your mirrors and/or glance behind before moving up to the overtake position, compromising your safe following distance for minimal time. Make sure a vehicle behind is not about to overtake, and that no-one is already coming up on the outside, possibly only visible to you with a proper shoulder check. Operate the right-hand indicator and select a lower gear if necessary for stronger acceleration, then ease out to a path that will allow you to overtake in a straight line. The gear you choose will ideally get you through the manoeuvre before you need to change up.

You will ease across to your overtaking line generally without accelerating and before you pass the tail of the vehicle ahead. This gives you a final opportunity to check the road ahead, including the nearside area that may have been hidden earlier. If you judge this movement accurately, you can postpone your manoeuvre, if you have to, simply by dropping back into place without having to brake. If everything looks safe, accelerate firmly.

Constant awareness is essential. As you position for the overtake, watch for the driver ahead changing course for no apparent reason, or even suddenly deciding to overtake the next vehicle ahead. Make sure the driver has seen you and knows your intention to pass: your horn can give valuable warning, but at higher speeds the average motorcycle horn is inaudible to a driver, especially one listening to the radio, and a headlight flash is of more use.

Wet weather

Overtaking obviously becomes more dangerous in bad conditions. The road surface is more treacherous, and spray thrown up by traffic reduces visibility.

The reasonable view ahead available when you lie back waiting to overtake can become obscured by a cloud of spray just at the point where you are most vulnerable, close behind the vehicle in front on an overtaking course.

Courtesy and consideration

When traffic is heavy, motorcyclists can free themselves from frustrating delay by making their way past strings of slow or stationary vehicles. It is vital that this process is done safely and courteously, and you must constantly be alert to the possibility of pedestrians and cars suddenly appearing through gaps in the traffic.

Speed must be kept right down to allow for other road users crossing what seems to them to be a row of stationary vehicles, and perhaps not even looking your way. You must also watch for drivers pulling out of a line of slow-moving or stationary traffic in order to turn right or even make a U-turn. They might well do so without checking behind because they assume that all the traffic behind has stopped too, completely forgetting about the existence of motorcycles.

All this means that the motorcyclist must proceed past a line of vehicles very slowly, with great care and preferably on the offside. If you are passing a jam with a view to turning left at a junction, it is permissible to make careful use of the clear space on the nearside.

Cross-hatchings

There are some cross-hatchings that are clearly defined as no-go areas by law and these must be avoided at all times in the course of your normal riding. Those bounded by solid white lines – to separate traffic or mark the approach to motorway slip roads – should never be encroached upon except in a serious emergency or if directed there by a police officer.

Thankfully the old three-lane 'killer' road layouts have been superseded nearly everywhere, either by double white line systems governing traffic or by hatched central strips to separate the vehicle streams. These strips are often bounded by broken lines, a subject on which the *Highway Code* gives guidance.

Rule 86 states: 'Areas of white diagonal stripes or white chevrons painted on the road are to separate traffic lanes or to protect traffic turning right. Where the marked area is bordered by an unbroken white line you must not enter it except in an emergency. Where the line is broken, you should not enter unless you can see that it is safe to do so.'

On many of our congested roads it makes sense to use the sanction implied in the last sentence to make progress when other less manoeuvrable vehicles are unable to do so. You should only attempt this at a moderate pace and in such a way that the drivers you pass are not inconvenienced or surprised.

A cross-hatched central strip bordered by broken lines can be used for overtaking, provided it is not defining a right-turn lane at a junction. Note this rider's use of a nearside position to extend the view through this right-hander.

Advanced checklist

- Make sure you always overtake safely, when plenty of time is available to complete the manoeuvre.

- Do not overtake when approaching a side turning or pedestrian crossing.

- Overtaking procedure: check behind, signal and engage a lower gear if necessary before easing out; make a final check on conditions ahead, then commit yourself using firm but smooth acceleration on a straight course; do not cut in sharply at the end of the manoeuvre.

- Take great care when passing slow-moving or stationary traffic, and do so on the offside unless you plan to turn left; be prepared for drivers who fail to check behind before pulling out of the stream to make a turn.

What the examiner looks for

- Is the build-up to overtaking carried out in a considered and planned way?

- Is the overtaking manoeuvre itself executed safely and decisively?

- Do you maintain the right distance from other vehicles, and use the mirror, signals and gears correctly?

- Bearing in mind the road, traffic and weather conditions, do you use overtaking opportunities to make good progress?

Junctions

The special care needed at junctions

Extra risks face motorcyclists wherever roads meet and converge, whether at crossroads, T-junctions, roundabouts or forks. A study by the Transport Research Laboratory has shown that 78 per cent of motorcycle accidents causing injury involve other vehicles, and that 68 per cent of these occur at junctions or roundabouts.

Accidents do not 'just happen'. They are caused by the mistakes made by all road users. You must recognise that they present an ideal opportunity for other road users to cause particular trouble for the motorcyclist. Be on your guard, therefore, for 'accidents waiting to happen'.

Crossing another stream of traffic when turning right is one of the extra hazards you face at junctions. Two-thirds of motorcycle accidents involving other vehicles occur at junctions.

By using the techniques of advanced motorcycling and applying a systematic approach, junctions can be dealt with as safely as any other part of the road system.

Crossroads and T-junctions

When you are approaching on the minor route, or when neither route has precedence, brake and change down so that you are ready to stop (even though signs may tell you only to give way) and pay attention to your positioning. Take up the correct position at an early stage after checking behind and signalling if necessary. If there is a 'stop' sign, you must actually come to a halt and put a foot down.

If there are no lane markings, position yourself positively as you approach and arrive at the junction. If you want to turn left, you should be close to the nearside. If you want to turn right, you should be close to the centre line. If you are at a crossroads and want to go straight ahead, you should take up a suitable position somewhere in the middle so that other drivers understand your intentions.

Position yourself close to the centre line when you want to turn right.

Position yourself close to the nearside when you want to turn left.

Never be taken in by this scenario. The driver of this car has left the indicator on but is clearly not making the turn.

While you wait for a break in the traffic, always be aware of a common cause of accidents. A vehicle approaching from your right and signalling left appears to be telling you that it will turn into your road, allowing you to move away. But indicators can be left on by mistake, or the driver, unaware that a confusing message is being given, may be planning to pull in immediately after passing your junction. Never assume that the vehicle will turn until you actually see the driver moving into another road. The only reliable information obtained from a flashing indicator is that the bulb is working.

Using the more major of the two routes at a crossroads does not entitle you to ride as you like. A driver may still make an unsignalled, sudden turn in front of you, or may slow down abruptly. Someone waiting to pull out from a side road may do so in front of you.

Show courtesy and consideration to other road users, but not so excessively that you put politeness before practicality. By all means let someone out of a side turning if it is safe for you to do so, but it is foolish if you have to cause drivers behind you to brake. Misplaced courtesy can cause problems for other road users who are not expecting it.

Turning right at crossroads

Right turns at crossroads can be more complicated because of the confusion which arises with opposing traffic also waiting to turn right. Where there are no road markings, half of the country's drivers seem to favour passing offside-to-offside, the other half nearside-to-nearside.

The usual rule is to pass offside-to-offside. In other words, pass behind an opposing vehicle waiting to turn right. Do otherwise only when road markings or the junction layout dictate it. Passing round behind other traffic gives you a clear view ahead as you make your turn, whereas the nearside-to-nearside approach can force you to nose out blindly across the traffic stream. It is hardly surprising that so many accidents occur where traffic turns right.

Just because you have a clearer and relatively higher view from your motorcycle than most car drivers, never be tempted to cut across a junction – in a way which other road users will not be expecting – in order to nip through ahead of a stream of traffic.

In this situation, where two approaching riders want to turn right at the same time, never cut across ahead of the other bike.

The correct procedure at a crossroads. Turning behind the opposing bike...

...gives both riders an unimpeded view of the traffic streams they have to cross.

Traffic lights

Never take advantage of traffic light changes to try to nip through a junction and save yourself time. Trying rashly to save a few seconds puts yourself and pedestrians at risk. You should stop if you can reasonably do so when green changes to amber, and you must certainly never pass through the lights after amber has changed to red.

When you are stopped, keep an eye on the lights controlling routes crossing your path, and look for the first sign of vehicles stopping as their lights turn to amber, so that you have advance warning of when your lights are about to change – but do not use this observation to take liberties with the lights by moving away before they change to green. When passing through green lights, always look out for the driver who jumps the lights and turns across your bows at the last minute.

There is an increasing tendency for drivers of all vehicles to cross red lights. A recent Gatso photo sequence taken in London on a dual-carriageway shows no fewer than *seven* vehicles driving through *six* seconds after the lights turned red. Four of them were trucks. Any rider on the intersecting road who was going for a smart getaway when the lights changed to green would have stood no chance.

It is to be hoped that this worthwhile use of automatic cameras will act as a deterrent as they become more widely used. In the meantime you must keep your forward observation fully in play so that you can be ready for the inconsiderate law breakers. Use discretion even when the lights are green.

Advanced observation approaching traffic lights can help you make better progress. If you have a choice of lanes, take the 'lane of least resistance' – the one with less traffic in it. Poor lane discipline on urban dual-carriageways often means that the nearside lane is emptier.

When travelling in an outside lane on an urban dual-carriageway, pick up at an early stage road markings indicating that the lane can be shared by traffic going straight ahead and turning right. Good observation and an early lane-change prevent you being trapped behind right-turn traffic when you want to go straight on.

Since there is often insufficient warning of filter lights ahead, sooner or later on an unfamiliar road you will come up to a green left-turn or right-turn filter when you wish to go straight on. Failing to comply with a green filter light is now an offence, so you must take the turn dictated by the filter and retrace your route as soon as you can.

Roundabouts

Positioning and signalling are important at roundabouts, and you should strike the right balance between reserve and haste by making a decisive, safe entry into the traffic flow.

When traffic is light enough, it should be possible to enter a

Good forward observation of traffic already on a roundabout allows advanced riders to enter the flow with only a modest reduction in speed.

roundabout where visibility is good with only a modest reduction in speed, one sustained and gentle application of the brakes, and a change to a lower gear. During the approach an experienced rider assesses in advance the flow of traffic on the roundabout, so that the arrival can be judged perfectly in order to merge into a suitable gap in the traffic without harsh acceleration or braking, and without hesitation.

If traffic is heavy you will simply have to wait at the entry road for the right gap. Many drivers are clueless – or apathetic – about positioning and signalling on roundabouts, so do not assume that a vehicle will go where you expect.

Priority is sometimes given to a major route passing through a roundabout. For a rider in an unfamiliar area, the need to give way to traffic entering a roundabout can cause a moment's confusion, but the advanced rider's observation skills should always identify this well ahead.

Mini roundabouts

Mini roundabouts are used to control traffic where there is no room for the more conventional layout, or to give priority to intersecting roads without the need for traffic lights, usually because traffic is light most of the day.

The more effective mini roundabout has a convex centre circle and this will give you no trouble on two wheels provided you do not take a short cut over it. Articulated lorries will have driven over this area (their large turning circles usually give them no choice), and there will be tyre rubber and even diesel residues to make life interesting.

Less considerate or less affluent local authorities often delineate a mini roundabout with just a white circle at the centre of the crossing, but the same respect for the surface is needed. On two wheels you proceed in exactly the same way as for a normal roundabout, taking extra care in view of the reduced traffic separation there.

Signalling on roundabouts

On all normal roundabouts you should keep to the established procedure outlined in the *Highway Code* unless lane markings tell you to do differently.

If you plan to take the first exit, you should position your

Never neglect your own signalling on roundabouts, but allow for unpredictable and unsignalled behaviour from other vehicles.

bike towards the left kerb and signal a left turn on your approach, keeping the indicator going until you leave the roundabout.

If you plan to go more or less straight across, it is preferable to keep to the left on your approach and through the roundabout, signalling a left turn after you have passed the exit before the one you intend to take. Your forward observation and course selected will bring you into the left-hand lane in good time as you approach the roundabout, but if other traffic is slow-moving and congested you might be able to make better progress in the right-hand lane when you intend to go ahead. Here it is essential to give that shoulder check or lifesaver before committing yourself to your exit line, in case other cars have come with you.

When choosing an exit more than 180 degrees round the roundabout you will stay in the right-hand lane, signalling a turn in plenty of time. Again you must allow for the driver who has come with you on your nearside and wants the turning after the one you have chosen, so use mirrors and shoulder checks to best advantage.

Giving signals

The art of good signalling

Giving the correct signals at the right time and in the right way is an essential part of good motorcycling. Visible and audible signals are our main means of communication to warn others of our intentions and presence. A rider can also communicate with other road users by positioning and, with co-operation from them, a situation can be commanded.

The art of good signalling is a complex part of advanced motorcycling which requires practice as well as learning. The ground rules are simple: use only those signals described in the *Highway Code*. Do not make up your own signals or copy those adopted by other people. Even if a personal signalling device seems perfectly clear to you, it could be dangerously misleading to someone else.

Signals are used to inform other road users, not to give orders to them. A signal never gives you the right to make a move, such as a lane change on a dual-carriageway or motorway, on the assumption that others will give way. Police officers who deal with accidents are used to hearing the excuse, 'But I gave a signal', from the person who has caused the trouble.

Do not expect other road users to react in the right way to your correct signalling. Another driver may not see your signal, or interpret it correctly, or act on it sensibly. Since you can never be certain that others will recognise your intentions, always ride so that you can change your plans if your signals are ignored.

Remember to check all lights – brake light, indicators, rear light and headlight – frequently since vibration can considerably shorten the life of bulb filaments. It is sensible to carry spare bulbs stowed somewhere on your bike or in a pocket of your regular riding jacket.

Always use signals – in practice direction indicators are the most important – to keep other road users informed, but do not expect the right reaction from them.

Direction indicators

Most of the signals you make while riding involve direction indicators. Direction indicators are used not only when turning left and right, but also before changing your position on the road. Use them thoughtfully and in good time so that other road users know what you are doing and can take action accordingly.

The failure to give proper signals is one of the most common faults you see in day-to-day driving. As an advanced rider, make sure you are never guilty of this. Always use your direction indicators properly at junctions, at roundabouts, when overtaking and when pulling in at the side of the road.

Avoid thinking that a signal is unnecessary at quiet times of the day or night just because few people are about. At the same time, signals can be used over-

zealously. It is unnecessary to signal by rote at country lane junctions if you really are on your own. When driving along an urban road dotted with parked cars, there is no need to signal every time you prepare to pass one. In situations such as these, use your direction indicators intelligently when other drivers would benefit.

The motorcyclist's common mistake is forgetting to cancel the indicators after a turn, in spite of a warning light on the bike's instrument panel. If you own a bike equipped with indicators which cancel after a certain time interval, get to know their period so that you are not caught out by them stopping just when you most need them – on a busy roundabout for instance.

The advantages of computers to manage engine ignition and fuel injection have been extended to give more sophisticated signal monitoring. Nowadays some machines even incorporate time, distance and cornering detectors to vary the time before an indicator is automatically cancelled.

Hand signals

There are occasions when the advanced rider should consider using the two basic hand signals – an extended arm to indicate left and right turns. A hand signal is advisable when you are not certain that your direction indicator has been seen (such as in bright sunlight) or when you need to emphasise your intentions.

A likely instance occurs when you plan to turn off where two side roads are close to each other, and you want to make it clear which one you are going to take. A roundabout with several exits close together provides an opportunity for clarifying your intentions with a hand signal. A right-turn hand signal can be valuable to show that you are intending to turn right and are not just pulling out to pass a parked vehicle.

Remember also that these hand signals – as well as the upright palm signal indicating an intention to go straight ahead – can be useful to communicate your plans to a police officer controlling traffic at a junction.

Although you do not often see it used, the slowing-down signal – an up-and-down movement of the right arm with the palm facing downwards – can be useful to emphasise the intentions indicated by your brake light. The right time for this signal is when you think that the driver behind is

A hand signal can be useful to clarify your intentions. An example might occur when your plan to turn right could be misinterpreted as an intention simply to change course round a row of parked cars.

either too close or driving inattentively, and therefore might not realise that you are coming to a halt in traffic. The signal is particularly appropriate when you stop at a pedestrian crossing, since it warns drivers not to overtake as you slow down. At times when taking a hand off the bar might be dangerous, a quick dab on the brakes just to flash the brake light can be used.

Most modern motorcycles make signalling with the right arm difficult because the twist grip winds back when you remove your hand, but engine braking is often appropriate when you need to give a hand signal.

Although there is a school of thought which believes that the hands are better employed on the handlebars than in signalling, occasional use of hand signals is a valuable aid to safety, as long as you do not ride one-handed for a moment longer than necessary.

Misplaced courtesy

Two hand signals are now omitted from the *Highway Code*, although some motorcyclists – and drivers – use them in the belief that they are being courteous to other road users. These are the 'You can overtake me' wave to a following vehicle and the 'Please cross' gesture to pedestrians on a crossing.

The problem with these is that if you make a mistake you could be guilty of causing an accident through your good intentions. It is not always possible for you to judge, from your position on your bike, whether others – drivers or pedestrians – can safely accept your invitation. Leave them to make their own judgement.

Since irresponsible drivers seem increasingly willing to break the law by overtaking on either side of traffic halted at a pedestrian crossing, the consequences of someone stepping into the road at your request could be extremely serious.

Inviting pedestrians to cross can expose them to danger that you have not seen – leave others to make their own decisions.

The headlight

The IAM recommends that motorcyclists should normally ride with the dipped headlight switched on. More than one-third of all accidents involving injury to motorcyclists occur because the other driver did not see the motorcycle, since bike and rider are relatively inconspicuous on roads dominated by cars, vans and lorries. Keeping the headlight on is compulsory in many countries.

Some experienced riders dislike daytime use of the headlight because they see it as the responsibility of other road users to look out for motorcyclists, but our experience indicates that a bike is more easily seen

Riding on dipped headlight makes you more conspicuous.

when its headlight is illuminated. There are so many drivers with inadequate concentration or defective vision (as well as short-sighted or careless pedestrians) that motorcyclists should use every aid to visibility at their disposal. There is no point in being theoretically in the right after an accident has occurred.

Keeping the headlight on in daylight also removes the temptation to imitate those confusing games drivers play with their headlights. Some flash their headlights to say 'Don't move, I'm coming through', while others use exactly the same signal to mean 'Although I'm on the main road I'm slowing down to let you out'. Headlight flashing should be used only in accordance with the *Highway Code*, as a warning to draw people's attention to your presence.

One *caveat* to the use of the headlight in daytime is necessary. You must ensure that you use dipped beam, and that your headlight is correctly adjusted in the vertical plane, or you will find you are riding in company with frustrated drivers who are dazzled by the reflection of your light in their mirrors. Worse still, a main headlight beam in daylight makes it very difficult for other road users to judge the distance you are from them.

Dipped headlight, conspicuous clothing and other aids to letting others know you are sharing the roads with them are all secondary or passive safety precautions, but they will not prevent the 'SmIdsy' situation ('Sorry, mate, I didn't see you') from happening. The principal benefit of advanced riding technique is that you can use it as a primary or active safety aid to defend yourself from the actions of other road users and to reduce the effects of adverse road conditions.

The brake light

Your brake light cannot be misunderstood by anybody: it works automatically and the message is totally clear. The

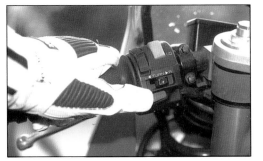

An early dab of the brakes can give advance warning to a driver following too closely behind.

advanced rider, however, can use the brake light thoughtfully to convey additional information to following drivers.

If you consider that a vehicle is sitting too close to your tail, it is useful when approaching a hazard to brake lightly at first to give the driver time to drop back to a safe distance before you have to brake more firmly. At times when taking a hand off the handlebar to give a slowing-down hand signal might be dangerous, an early dab of the brakes can give the necessary warning to drivers behind.

The horn

The horn should be sounded when it is necessary to inform other road users of your presence. It should be used sparingly, but you should not be reluctant to use it firmly at the right time as it can be a life-saver. It is illegal, except in an emergency to avoid an accident, to sound your horn between 11.30pm and 7.00am in a built-up area or at any time of day or night if your bike is stationary.

There are three situations when using the horn should be considered. First, it can serve as warning of your approach when the view ahead is very limited, perhaps when nearing a dangerous crossroads where the side roads are obscured by

Do not ignore the horn. Occasions occur when thoughtful and courteous use of it is helpful.

hedges. Second, the horn can be valuable when another road user is vulnerable despite all your safety precautions – cyclists, pedestrians and children might all benefit. Third, a firm but polite note on the horn can be used when you are about to overtake another vehicle whose driver may not have noticed you – this is often appropriate when passing a large truck or tractor.

Never use the horn, however, as a substitute for the observation, planning and courtesy which are the mark of a good motorcyclist. Remember that British drivers seem far more ready than Europeans to take offence at the sound of a horn, so use it with discretion. If a note on the horn is not delivered 'politely', some take it as a reprimand, a challenge or an insult, and react accordingly.

Thoughtful and courteous use of the horn is what counts. You may not use it often, but to believe that it should never be used is a mistake. Treat it as the action of last resort to protect your own position.

Roadcraft in town

Concentration in town

Busy conditions in town demand impeccable observation. Visible amid the congestion here are a taxi pulling across the traffic, a bus stopping ahead, a pedestrian walking across in front of the white van, three sets of lights and an impatient dispatch rider.

Riding in built-up areas demands sustained concentration and a high degree of observation. Traffic is heavier, situations change more quickly, buildings and vehicles restrict views, and the frequency of road junctions creates many more accident possibilities.

Local knowledge is invaluable in town, although you must always guard against dropping your level of concentration simply because you are riding in familiar territory. Whenever the advanced motorcyclist ventures to unfamiliar places, however, their features are consciously recorded in order to remember important junctions, badly congested areas, one-way systems, roundabouts and filter lights. The more that can be memorised, the more familiar the route will be next time.

Whether or not you are riding over known roads, keep trying to observe what is happening to the traffic flow ahead by positioning yourself carefully to maximise your view.

Watch for the pattern of junctions coming up and get in the correct line of traffic well in advance. If you find yourself stuck in the wrong lane and cannot safely move to the right one, you have no alternative but to keep to your committed path and use your sense of direction to find your way back to the right road.

An example of advanced roadcraft in town: the red car is being used as a shield when pulling out into traffic from rest.

Route observation

Shrewd observation often provides you with valuable snippets of information which a less skilled rider would miss. Remind yourself about the points of selective observation covered on page 26.

Keeping an eye on large lorries or buses well down a line of traffic can give you early warning of a halt. Look ahead for bus-stop signs and note passengers crowding towards the doors of a bus ready to get off. Always be prepared for taxis to move off, stop suddenly or make a U-turn, especially if the 'hire' sign is lit and the cab might be hailed. Shopping streets and railway stations are places where you need to be particularly vigilant for unexpected actions from taxi drivers.

Lines of parked cars always present potential hazards for motorcyclists. Treat a car with special care if you can see an occupant who may throw open a door in your path, and watch for the tell-tale signs – a driver at the wheel, a puff of smoke or vibration from the exhaust, reversing lights illuminated or front wheels angling out – which reveal that a car may be about to pull out.

Two of many hazards you can face when riding in town. A door can open when passing a line of parked cars (above). Hazard warning lights (left) can cause confusion if only the right-hand indicator is visible, although here alert observation picks up the left-hand one through the silver car's window.

Pedestrians

Pedestrians are another potential hazard. Lines of parked cars or stationary traffic are places where a pedestrian may pop through a gap without expecting a motorcyclist to be coming. The advanced rider will be very careful where shoppers may step off a pavement, or near particular buildings – schools, factories or railway stations – where many people may be present at certain times of day.

Special care is needed where pedestrians cross at traffic lights. People often step into the road when they hear the 'green man' bleeping without glancing to see whether it is actually safe to do so. When a crowd of pedestrians streams across in front of you, it is quite possible that a few 'stragglers' will cross as your lights are changing to green.

The motorcyclist must always be alert for pedestrians unexpectedly crossing the road, perhaps to take advantage of a gap in the traffic without looking carefully enough to notice your presence. Watch for small movements – a turn of the head, a brisk walk towards the kerb or a wave of recognition – which may give a clue to a pedestrian's next move.

Cyclists

Give cyclists plenty of room when you pass, as they may lack your road sense and make sudden movements. Beware of the cyclist who emerges from a side street without looking, and never forget that any cyclist is entitled to a wobble, as a High Court ruling has confirmed. It is the motorcyclist's responsibility to avoid a cyclist.

As a rider you know the benefits of filtering through traffic, but always check behind. A cyclist can do this even more effectively than you.

As well as cyclists, some motorcyclists have to be watched – this one has a shopping bag hanging from the right handlebar.

Filtering

When traffic is very heavy, the motorcyclist can often take advantage of room to thread past lines of slow-moving or stationary vehicles, but such opportunities should be taken only when gaps are wide enough to be negotiated safely.

Watch very carefully for pedestrians who will not be expecting you, and for the few bad-tempered drivers who show their resentment of the motorcyclist's greater freedom by deliberately trying to block your path. Fall back into line when in doubt, and wait patiently for safe overtaking opportunities to present themselves again.

Filter through traffic slowly and unobtrusively, mindful of the possibility of pedestrians appearing in your path.

Lane discipline

Lane discipline is vital in the one-way systems used in many larger towns to keep traffic moving.

In really congested conditions which encourage drivers to become more forceful, or even aggressive, motorcyclists have to be especially careful to look ahead and notice turns out of the system in time to take up position among a stream of nose-to-tail cars in the appropriate lane. Keep to the left, unless this lane leads to a mandatory left turn you do not want to follow, or you plan to turn right.

Overtaking is permissible on both sides on one-way streets, but if you pass vehicles on the nearside be alert to the possibility of some of them suddenly moving into your path in order to turn left. Watch out for pedestrian crossings in one-way streets, as these can often be almost completely obscured by congested traffic.

Road surfaces

Urban streets are usually more slippery than country roads because the coating of oil and rubber becomes polished by constant traffic. Special care is needed even in dry weather, but after a shower urban roads can become treacherous.

Oil tends to accumulate on the road at any places where vehicles stop regularly, such as at traffic lights, so allow for the possibility of greatly reduced grip when braking and accelerating. Tight junctions, roundabouts and filling stations are places where you may encounter spilled diesel fuel.

Remember, too, that dense traffic can give you less freedom to avoid common surface irregularities, such as drains, manhole covers, potholes and puddles.

Traffic lights

Leave a bigger gap when stopped on a hill in case the vehicle ahead drops back.

When you stop at traffic lights, you should always select neutral, release the clutch lever and cover the brakes while waiting for the lights to change. This avoids unnecessary clutch wear and removes the danger of the sudden jerk forward which would occur if your left hand slipped while in gear.

For the same reasons, holding your bike stationary on a hill by slipping the clutch is bad practice. If you have stopped on a hill, always allow a little extra room in case the vehicle in front should roll back. The driver may not have applied the handbrake firmly, or may make such a clumsy start that the vehicle rolls back before the clutch bites.

Confidence in congested conditions

Motorcyclists and drivers who are used to the very dense, sometimes fast-moving traffic of large cities are generally more confident. London riders and drivers, in particular, have a decisive style which seems almost foolhardy to people from quieter parts of the country, but by and large it works well because they know what they are doing and where they are going. The 'press-on' approach helps to keep large volumes of traffic moving through some very congested road systems.

There can be no more vivid illustration of this style than the behaviour of dispatch riders in large cities. Before dismissing them all as hooligans, it is worth remembering that

Dispatch riders can display reckless tendencies, but there is a lesson in their forceful approach – riding in congested conditions requires decisiveness.

anyone earning a living on a bike has to stay in one piece. Some of their manoeuvres would produce an immediate failure in the Advanced Motorcycling Test, but the skill of top-class dispatch riders cannot be denied, especially as 30,000 to 50,000 miles a year is common for them.

Your riding should be in keeping with your surroundings. Applying a decisive style to gaps in the traffic when riding in a provincial town can seem aggressive, even downright dangerous, partly because it is out of place. In the same way, someone riding warily in London for the first time must try not to be intimidated by the cut-and-thrust of somewhere like Hyde Park Corner in the rush hour. Each type of progress is right for the conditions, so it can be dangerous if you do not – or even feel that you cannot – conform to the traffic pattern around you.

Roadcraft in the country

Riding on open roads

Although the basic rules of advanced motorcycling remain the same in all environments, riding on open roads needs a completely different set of roadcraft abilities. Country roads with little traffic give the motorcyclist a chance to use riding skills to the full, and to enjoy the pleasure of taking bends at speed and with pleasing rhythm.

Your need to assess the road ahead is just as important in the country as in town, but the clues are different. The list is almost endless, but one hallmark of the advanced rider is the ability to sift useful information from everything that can be seen. A few examples can illustrate the point so that you become skilled in practising selective and shrewd observation.

To cover the intricacies of every possible situation is beyond the scope of any book, so this section is intended to show the types of problem encountered, to give you some basic clues to help you refine your abilities, and to encourage you to meet the high standards of roadcraft needed to pass the Advanced Motorcycling Test.

Canals and railways, even though disused, may mean hump-back bridges are not far away. A line of telegraph poles ahead can indicate the severity of a hidden bend, but do not rely on this since telegraph poles can track straight on when a road bends. Any livestock in the fields would suggest that you should watch for mud and slime on the road near any gateways or farms. The lie of trees and hedges can indicate the steepness of any incline. Isolated houses are points where you need to take extra care in case people or animals appear.

Full advantage should be taken of views of stretches of road visible in the distance.

Alert observation gives you early notice of any unusual road patterns ahead, such as a hump-back bridge over a canal or railway.

Sometimes you can string together enough glimpses of the road ahead to spot an overtaking opportunity that most riders would miss. You can also give yourself early warning of a wide lorry approaching on a narrow road if you see it through a gap in the trees, or of a car on a converging side road if you notice it briefly through a gateway or a gap in the trees.

Any special features you remember could be useful on another journey over the same route, so take note of bad patches of surface, deceptive bends and unexpected hazards.

Road surfaces

Country road surfaces, particularly on smaller roads, can present many surprises.

The combination of a series of bends between high walls or hedges can conceal all manner of dangers, such as potholes, mud, patches of ice, deep puddles, streams of water across the road, tightening bends, dead animals, wet leaves and a strange variety of cambers and bumps.

Knowing your route

Any long journey on country roads is more enjoyable, and safer, if you have prepared your route in advance. All your concentration is available for safe riding if you do not have to search for signposts, worry about getting lost or make frequent stops to check a map.

It is a good idea to memorise your route before you leave home, or make notes of landmark towns, villages and junctions on a piece of card which can be stuck to the top of your fuel tank.

Safe stopping distances

The lack of traffic on country roads can tempt even experienced riders into travelling too fast for safety, so always be sure to ride at a speed which allows you to stop within the distance you can see. Expect a tractor or a herd of cows around every blind bend.

Be careful, too, to maintain a safe stopping distance when following other vehicles. Some riders are prone to pressing too close, particularly if they generally ride in urban areas where speeds are lower and safe braking distances are shorter.

Keep a proper braking distance even if you are overtaken, and do not fall into the trap of allowing an inadequate distance just because you can see round or over the car in front. Just occasionally, perhaps if another car emerges suddenly from a side road, the vehicle in front will brake more quickly than you expect. Since so few car drivers leave a safe distance, do not take the gap left by others as some sort of standard for yourself.

Always expect the unexpected on quiet country roads. The proximity of farm buildings suggests that a muddy entrance could lie just beyond this speed limit sign.

Technique on dual-carriageways

The experienced rider shows good lane discipline on dual-carriageways with two or three lanes. You will use the nearside lane unless overtaking, but when traffic is busy you may spend much of your time in the centre or outside lanes.

Although these roads usually have the same 70mph speed limit as motorways, you often encounter an added range of hazards, such as side turnings to the left without slip roads, traffic slowing down in the outside lane in order to turn right, and slow-moving vehicles such as tractors or milk-floats.

It is not worth seeking the fastest convoys by moving from one lane to another on a busy road: each lane change is an unnecessary danger and frequently offers no advantage.

4 ADVANCED RIDING IN DIFFICULT CONDITIONS

Riding at night

Visibility

Considerations of road surface, safe stopping distance and dazzle all affect riding at night, but observation possibilities can increase.

Remember to apply that basic rule of good motorcycling – always travel at a speed which enables you to stop within the distance you can see – when riding at night. This means keeping your speed down so that you can always pull up safely within the distance illuminated by your headlight.

On dipped beam along a straight road this may mean that your speed has to be lower at night than during the day. When switching from main to dipped beam, reduce your speed if necessary to a level appropriate to your shorter range of visibility. If you find your speed creeping up, remind yourself of the road surface hazards which could lie just beyond the pool of light from your dipped headlight.

You need to be aware constantly of the state of the road surface. This means riding on main beam whenever you are on an empty road, although the concentration of light from dipped beam can be preferable for picking out the nearside of the road when rounding left-hand bends. Be very cautious when the road surface is bad, and remember that the central position of a motorcycle headlight creates a temptation to ride directly at a suspicious object or patch of road to illuminate it better.

But riding at night is not all about extra difficulties: it definitely has its advantages. When traffic begins to thin out, a journey can become quicker and less stressful. Out in the country the ability to see other vehicles, street lighting or even lights from a distant house can give you a 'bigger' picture of the conditions around you. On a twisty road the light thrown by oncoming vehicles gives you early warning of their approach and can help you to assess a bend before you reach it. The extra observation possibilities at night can also allow you to create more overtaking opportunities.

At the same time, however, you must resist the temptation to drop your guard during an exhilarating night-time ride. It can be difficult to judge speed and distance, so oncoming vehicles can sometimes be very much closer and travelling more quickly than you think. Remember, too, the possibility of misjudgement from other drivers: compared with a car, a motorcycle's single headlight (or closely paired headlights) makes assessing speed and distance more difficult. Sooner or later you will encounter an oncoming driver overtaking recklessly because your approach has been misjudged.

Do not join that curious breed of British drivers who think that dipped headlights should be used with the greatest reluctance, and that parking lights are perfectly adequate for driving around town. Always use your dipped headlight, day and night, town and country, to emphasise your presence. In bad weather or towards dusk, your headlight is particularly valuable in helping others to judge the speed of your approach, for a motorcycle can become practically invisible in such conditions when running without lights or on parking light only. In built-up areas your dipped headlight also helps you to pick up road surface abnormalities which might not be revealed by the uneven cast of street lights.

On damp winter roads it is surprising how quickly mud can coat your headlight. Just think how often you need to clean your goggles or visor, and then imagine the layer of dirt which your headlight is trying to pierce.

Dazzle

Inexperienced riders sometimes find it difficult to cope with glare from the headlights of oncoming vehicles. Make a conscious effort to look away and concentrate your gaze on your side of the road. With experience this reaction becomes second nature, and you start to appreciate oncoming headlights for the extra light which they throw into your path.

One problem on open roads is that a few thoughtless motorists fail to dip their lights when a motorcyclist approaches, although dipping your own beam in good time usually brings the right response. By all means use a quick flash on to main beam to remind a driver to dip, but never be tempted to stay on main beam in order to retaliate. Two dazzled road users are twice as dangerous as one.

Remember how the human eye works if you become dazzled. While it can quickly contract the pupil to shut out unwanted light, it takes much longer to dilate afterwards. For several seconds after a vehicle on main beam has passed by, you may be riding with significantly reduced vision.

Eyesight and fatigue

Sight deficiencies can be relatively worse at night, so make sure your eyes are tested regularly by an optician. Your visor or goggles must be in good condition and kept clean, since any scratch, speck of dirt or smear of grease will distort and reflect light, making the task of night observation even harder.

Travelling any distance after dark is undoubtedly more tiring than daylight riding. Fatigue makes itself felt first as eye strain caused by looking along the headlight beam, avoiding being dazzled by the lights of other vehicles and keeping your powers of observation razor-sharp.

You can help to reduce the risk of tiredness by trying to avoid making a long journey at night after a strenuous day. A snack before starting is better than a heavy meal, which might make you feel drowsy. Certainly keep off all alcohol. Heavier clothing will be needed to keep you warm in lower night-time temperatures, not just for comfort but also to keep your circulation and reaction times at normal levels.

Keep asking yourself whether you feel at all tired, and stop for a break if you do.

Stretch your arms and legs, and rest your eyes. You could even go for a short but vigorous run up the road to get your circulation going again. Carrying a flask of hot coffee or tea can help to restore your senses when a break is necessary.

The monotony of motorways at night can lead to fatigue and poor concentration, so stop at service areas or junctions when you need to. Changing your cruising speed from time to time to vary the engine note, vibration and wind pressure can also help you to stay alert.

Your motorcycle's lights

Most motorcycles are now equipped with a powerful quartz-halogen headlight which throws a reasonably long and intense beam, but those fitted with old-fashioned tungsten filaments can give you an inadequate view at night. If you are unhappy about the lighting of tungsten bulbs on your machine, it would be sensible to investigate a quartz-halogen conversion. As long as your bike's alternator or generator has the capacity to cope with the bigger power demand, it should be possible to fit a complete light assembly into the headlight shell.

One aspect of motorcycle design, rear lighting, falls far behind accepted standards for cars. Only a few makes of motorcycle incorporate high-intensity rear foglights, and few rear mudguards or tail fairings will easily accept an auxiliary light unit. Even so, if much winter or night riding is contemplated, every effort should be made to fit a suitable lamp. The types sold for trailers or caravans, often described as 'bulkhead fitting', are usually the easiest to adapt for motorcycle use.

A motorcycle's vibration makes all light bulbs prone to failure, and obviously you have a serious problem if the headlight or rear light fails at night. Carry spare bulbs with you all the time, making sure you wrap them well (if you carry them in a pocket) so that fragments of broken glass cannot cut you if you fall off. Check the rear light and brake light from time to time during a long journey, and look over the condition of wiring, snap connectors and terminals before setting out. Wiring might fray or a connector separate, particularly on an older machine.

Riding in winter

Wet roads

Anti-lock brakes on this Yamaha FJ1200 help this rider to cope with a streaming wet surface.

Rain is the most common problem for the motorcyclist in winter. Constant caution and sensitive use of the controls are required on slippery road surfaces and in poor visibility. Corners should be taken more slowly to prevent skidding and braking should be gentle, with the emphasis on the rear brake and the engine's retarding effect.

Try to keep well clear of other vehicles, especially when speeds rise. You need more room for braking, and spray thrown up by other vehicles makes judging speed and distance more difficult. Cars tend to mist up in bad weather and the way drivers concentrate on the view ahead can make them less attentive to motorcycles behind or to either side.

Spray also coats your goggles or visor, either of which are prone to misting up on the inside in winter weather. This can be prevented by applying one of the anti-mist products available from accessory shops or by rubbing the surface with washing-up liquid.

Spray thrown up by heavy vehicles obscures visibility on wet roads, especially at higher speeds.

Icy roads

In freezing conditions it is vital to read the road meticulously so that you anticipate dangerous spots before they catch you out.

If you really cannot avoid riding in snow, go about it with extreme care. The dangers are self-evident and you need to be very cautious in the use of braking and acceleration. In practice the most hazardous conditions can occur when snow turns to slush and traffic around you starts to move more quickly. Cars can slice reasonably easily through ridges of slush between wheel tracks, but these conditions are very tricky for the motorcyclist whenever course changes are required.

Frost is heaviest late into the night and in the early morning, so the risks are reduced in cold weather if you can make a journey later during the day or in early evening. Try to keep to main roads which have been salted or gritted, and to an extent scoured by traffic, since minor roads may not have been treated in the same way.

An indirect result of gritting is that the fine layer of gravel deposited on the road is soon worked towards the verge by traffic, so it can be wise to ride nearer the kerb where the surface is less likely to be icy.

Even on a fine day when the road surface seems normal, ice can linger where trees and walls shade the road, where gradients are not warmed by the sun, or where wind sweeps across an exposed hilltop or bridge.

Although the roughened texture of concrete road surfaces with lateral grooves can offer good grip in dry weather, water which settles in these grooves can create a very treacherous surface when it freezes.

Expert observation of the road surface is absolutely crucial when dealing with isolated patches of frozen road, but keep an eye on other road users as well since their actions can give you advance warning of danger in icy conditions.

Conditions become very hazardous for the motorcyclist as snow turns to slush, especially when traffic around you starts to move more quickly.

Black ice

The notorious hazard of black ice should always be expected on a cold night, and for several hours at least during the following morning. Black ice occurs where water has melted during the day and frozen again as the temperature drops after dusk. The road surface looks wet when in fact is is icy – and in some conditions black ice can be virtually invisible.

Because black ice occurs in patches, it is very easy to be lulled into a sense of false security after riding for several miles along a road which seems normal. The only advice must be to ride very, very gingerly when the temperature is low enough for black ice to be a risk.

Bike maintenance

Some of the accessories that can be useful in winter (right), and an example of the frame corrosion (far right) that can be minimised by frequent washing.

It is important to keep your motorcycle in good shape to carry you through the winter. Grip is your first priority, so make sure your tyres have plenty of tread and no sidewall damage, and check the pressures regularly.

Electrical systems are tested severely in winter. The battery must be in good condition to cope with starting on cold mornings, and the short daylight hours mean that heavy demands are made on lighting systems. Damp plug leads and connectors can cause uneven engine running during winter, since water can work its way under connectors to short out spark plugs during heavy rain, this dampness lingering for days afterwards to cause intermittent misfiring.

Corrosion can be reduced by frequent washing to remove salt and road dirt, and paintwork benefits from regular waxing. Some motorcyclists like to coat wheels, engine castings and parts of the frame with grease or WD-40 to repel salt and water, and then clean off this protective (but messy) layer with solvent when spring comes.

Keeping warm

Pan-European Honda ST1100 has touring fairing ideal for winter riding.

Cold weather is as hard on the rider as on the machine. As well as making sure your protective clothing keeps you warm enough (see pages 11-13), build in enough time on a long journey to make frequent stops to warm up and stretch cold limbs. It is impossible to work the controls quickly and sensitively if your hands and feet are numb. Coldness soon exhausts your whole body, slowing down your reactions and impairing concentration.

A fairing improves comfort in winter by diverting cold air, rain and spray. If your machine lacks a fairing, consider having one fitted but do not overlook the possible problems. Although the disadvantages vary with the machine and type of fairing, they include reduced steering lock and fitting difficulties, the latter perhaps involving repositioning of instruments, handlebars, controls, headlight, wiring and indicators.

When buying a new machine you are inevitably influenced by style, but pay attention to practicality. Many sports fairings look exciting but fail to give much protection for your hands.

Advanced checklist

- When roads are slippery, use your bike's controls – brakes, throttle, clutch – even more smoothly and gently than normal to avoid skidding, keeping the emphasis on the rear brake.

- Read the road to prepare yourself for slippery spots; treat the surface with the utmost respect if black ice is a possibility.

- Make sure both you and your machine are prepared for winter; keep your visor (or goggles) clean on the outside and demisted on the inside.

What the examiner looks for

- Do you keep a good eye on the road surface, especially in bad weather?

- Does your motorcycle appear to be properly maintained?

- Are you adequately dressed for cold weather conditions?

Riding in summer

Road surfaces

After the perils of riding in winter, all motorcyclists cheer up at the thought of the dry roads, long hours of daylight, good visibility and warm air which come with summer. But summer can present difficult road surfaces too.

A film of dust, rubber and oil accumulates on roads during dry weather. While this does not greatly affect grip while the road remains dry, a summer shower or morning dew can make this greasy coating very slippery. The longer a spell without rain, the more treacherous the roads can be when rain does come, particularly at points where traffic is heavy.

On a very hot day the road surface can heat up to a point where tarmac beings to melt. A stretch of road where the surface appears to have a sheen may not offer as much grip as usual, particularly if traffic is heavy. Sometimes you see signs of the surface breaking up on bends under the pressure of heavy lorries, so remember that grip will be reduced on this bumpy, slightly sticky surface.

Summer is also the time of 'loose chippings'. Dressed with tar and stones, such roads need to be treated cautiously because grip is reduced and stones are thrown up by other vehicles. After a while the surface begins to bed down, but even so you must remember that loose stones tend to accumulate at the edge of the road, creating a surface akin to riding on marbles.

Other summer factors

On a motorcycle you can escape some of the congestion on holiday routes during school breaks and over bank holiday weekends, but you cannot escape the antics of drivers around you. These are situations where you see plenty of very poor driving.

The typical holiday driver is hot and bothered, unused to long journeys, frustrated by delay, distracted by fractious children, and unable to see properly out of an overloaded car. Expect the unexpected.

The temptation to ride wearing light summer clothing – perhaps just a pair of shorts and a tee-shirt – should be resisted on a really hot day.

Summer rain

Summer showers or thunderstorms can be very heavy. Rather than ploughing on in greatly reduced visibility and without the sort of protection offered by winter clothing, it is invariably better to seek shelter until the rain has passed. The high humidity which accompanies summer thunderstorms can also make your visor or goggles mist up.

Rain can fall so quickly that large puddles can form at the edge of the road, perhaps where drains are blocked. If this looks likely, slow right down to a pace which allows you to cope if suddenly faced with several centimetres of water under your wheels.

Rain sometimes falls so heavily that roads become flooded in dips, although this occurs more often in winter when the ground is water-logged. Although car drivers might be able to negotiate a flooded road, the risk of unseen potholes and mud makes this unwise for the motorcyclist. You can also become immobilised if water splashed up by the front wheel finds its way into the electrics. If in any doubt, turn round and find another route along nearby back roads.

If you do decide to press on through standing water on a road whose visible surface looks good, proceed at a modest pace in low gear, taking care to keep engine revs up to avoid water being sucked back up the exhaust. Keep up an even pace – slipping the clutch if necessary to maintain a good engine speed – which is slow enough to prevent water from the front wheel spraying over the engine.

Once clear of the flood, dry out the brakes with several jabs on pedal and lever.

Watching a car's progress through standing water can tell you whether it is safe to proceed.

Riding in fog

Speed and vision

The fundamental rule in fog, as in all other conditions, is to keep your speed down to a level which allows you to stop within the range of your vision, even if this means travelling at only 10mph.

Riding at a slow, steady pace, you should use the nearside kerb or verge as the main guide to your position if you are alone in fog. White lines and cat's eyes can also show you where the road goes, but never let them encourage you into riding faster than your

vision allows. Never ride too close to the centre line as someone approaching might be doing the same.

While the limits of vision are the vital consideration, motorcyclists must never forget that fog is usually accompanied by a slippery, damp road surface, so your speed and use of the controls must take account of this.

Your goggles or visor must be kept clean by frequent wiping, as the droplets of water which form fog can accumulate without your noticing it. When riding very slowly in thick fog, you may obtain a clearer view by removing your eye protection.

When visibility is reduced, speed must be kept down to a level which enables you to stop within the distance you can see. If you are on a busy dual-carriageway or motorway, you may consider it safer to find a quieter route.

Being seen

Although the IAM recommends that you normally ride with your dipped headlight on, this becomes vital in fog. Never use the parking light alone as other drivers simply will not be able to spot you so easily.

It is better to avoid using main beam, because fog reflects so much light that dipped beam generally gives you a better view. Fog lamps, if you have them, are designed to give better light penetration in fog. Make sure your rear light is working and any mud thrown up by the rear wheel is

washed off before you start out on your journey.

Junctions are always hazardous in fog, particularly right turns, so flash your headlight on to main beam and sound your horn when you have to cross the path of other vehicles. You are at great risk while turning at a right angle across a road because your front and rear lights cannot be seen by an oncoming driver.

Besides all the usual careful observation, try to listen for the sound of an approaching vehicle when you are preparing to turn right in fog. Even with a helmet on you might be able to hear an approaching vehicle before you see it, especially at night.

Traffic

It is very easy in fog to think that a vehicle ahead of you is moving unnecessarily slowly. But remember that while you can see a pair of red beacons through the fog, the driver ahead may be able to see virtually nothing.

Never be tempted to overtake, since this puts you – and anyone who might be coming the other way – at great risk. You can also be misled about visibility because a vehicle ahead of you makes a slight 'hole' in the droplets of water which form fog. You may feel that the fog has eased slightly while you are in another vehicle's wake, only to find, when you are committed to an overtaking manoeuvre, that it is as thick as ever. Furthermore you may feel under pressure, once you are in front, to justify your manoeuvre to drivers pressing close behind by riding too fast for the conditions.

Instead, it is much better to keep station and keep calm.

While it is wise to stay in line, do not be tempted to say in touch with the tail lights of a driver whose speed seems too fast for safety. In the sense of loneliness which accompanies fog it can be reassuring to ride in the presence of other vehicles, giving your eyes some relief from the strain of peering through the gloom, but do so only in a manner which is safe for the conditions.

When you are following another vehicle, leave enough space to stop, remembering that the driver may not slow down and stop in the normal way. There is always the risk that the leader of a convoy will hit a crashed car and stop instantaneously.

Many drivers travel too fast and too close together in fog. If a driver overtakes and fills the safe space you have left, ease back to restore the correct distance. You can discourage motorists from squeezing past you by riding well out into the road, since having a car ahead to act as a 'pilot' reduces the need for you to use the nearside verge as a guide to your position. But do not impede impetuous drivers: let them by and then stay well out of their way.

In fog it can be reassuring to ride in company with other vehicles, giving your eyes relief from peering through the gloom – but always keep your distance and avoid hanging on to the tail lights of someone travelling too fast.

Patchy fog

Fog can occur in patches, sometimes unexpectedly. Pockets of fog sometimes linger in valleys on an undulating country road, even in summer. Sea fog can occur on coastal roads. If the cloudbase is low you can suddenly find yourself in fog on high ground. Fog tends to form first over areas of water, so if you see mist developing expect thicker patches where the road crosses a river.

Good observation should always prepare you for patches of fog. Drop your speed, make sure your dipped headlight is on and keep a sharp eye on traffic ahead of you.

5 ADVANCED MOTORWAY RIDING

Joining and leaving the motorway

Do you need to use a motorway?

Motorways sometimes have their attractions for the motorcyclist. After the congestion which goes with riding in towns or on busy trunk roads, the escape to an open stretch of motorway can raise your spirits as you wind up the engine to a comfortable cruising speed, look forward to making fast progress with no intersections, run on a smooth

Long motorway journeys become monotonous and stressful on a motorcycle. Ask yourself whether you need to use a motorway, or whether taking to normal trunk roads for part of the route might add variety.

surface and ride with a good view of the road ahead.

A couple of hours later you may feel differently, yearning for some 'real riding' on an old-fashioned trunk road. The continuous stress of high-speed riding, the stiffness of body and limbs which hardly change position, the constant speed and the unchanging noise add up to a feeling of fatigue and numbness of the mind which remind you that motorcycling on

motorways is not much fun.

Some of the rigours of motorway riding are reduced if you have a large-capacity bike designed for touring, but even on a comfortable, high-geared machine long stints on a motorway can be monotonous. It is important, therefore, to ask yourself before a journey whether you really want to ride on motorways and, if so, for how long?

Taking in a stretch of motorway can make a short trip quicker and more relaxed, but if you plan to make a longer journey which involves riding for most of the day it is worth trying to follow a route which mixes trunk roads and motorways. Many motorways run reasonably parallel to the trunk roads they were designed to supersede, so you can generally plot a route which uses a combination of both. A good plan is to use motorways to pass large towns and cities, but take to trunk roads for the sake of variety where these might offer some appealing ordinary road riding.

If you cannot avoid spending most of a long journey on the motorway, build in enough time to allow for regular stops to stretch your limbs and rest your mind.

Joining a motorway

The motorway slip road should be used to accelerate to a speed which matches that of traffic in the inside lane. Signal a right turn so that anyone in the inside lane will notice you, and maybe move over to the centre lane to give you plenty of room.

Your run along the stretch of slip road adjoining the main carriageway should be timed so

that you can slip neatly into place as soon as possible without losing speed, but keep a wary eye on the timid driver who may be slowing down at the end of the slip road to wait for a larger gap in the traffic. In extreme cases, this kind of driver – who is as much of a menace to himself as to other road users – may even stop at the end of the slip road as if to give way.

Joining a motorway needs first-rate rear observation to

Good rear observation is vital when joining a motorway. Certainly make a shoulder check, but consider a lifesaver if traffic ahead allows this longer look to the rear.

Try to choose the quieter lane when a slip road is divided by cross-hatchings. The solid border to these cross-hatchings means they must not be crossed except in an emergency.

assess the situation on the slip road as well as the motorway itself. Good mirror work is the basis, but as a minimum you should make a shoulder check just before you join the carriageway. Using the lifesaver on motorways is a contentious subject because of the distance you travel while looking behind, but it is a good precaution when you join the motorway. In heavy traffic make

sure circumstances ahead of you allow safe use of the lifesaver.

Advanced riding is all about total awareness, and you can find opportunities to plan your course even before venturing on the slip road. Your eye level is superior to that of most car drivers and you can use it to observe traffic patterns and flow. A good example is when the motorway is approached by a bridge or an embankment. If you assess traffic in advance correctly, you will find it easier to blend smoothly with it from the slip road.

Traffic on slip roads is increasingly segregated by strips of cross-hatching with a solid border. You must not cross these areas except in an emergency. Take up your position at an early stage, using the 'lane of least resistance' if you have a choice. Sometimes this might be the inside lane, which will join the motorway a good distance further on, but the outside lane is better if there are heavy lorries about.

You should remain in the inside lane until you have adjusted yourself to the speed and assessed the traffic pattern behind you. Your cruising speed will probably mean that you spend a good proportion of your motorway journey in the centre lane, so move over (after the usual rear observation and right-turn signal) when it becomes necessary. Return to the inside lane whenever it is reasonably clear after overtaking has been completed.

Leaving a motorway

When planning to leave a motorway, make sure you return to the inside lane at an early stage, certainly by the three-bar sign.

Junction signs are normally posted 1 mile and ½ mile in advance, followed by three-, two- and one-bar signs which provide a countdown starting at 300 yards. You must synchronise your speed with the traffic in the inside lane, making sure you have moved into this lane by the time you reach the three-bar sign, or earlier in heavy traffic. The right time to start your left-turn signal is at the three-bar sign.

Caution is needed on the slip road. After riding for maybe a couple of hours at close to the

legal limit, your judgement of speed will have become distorted. Since 50mph can seem more like 30mph, it is easy to approach the roundabout or junction at the end of the slip road too quickly and end up having to brake heavily. Some slip roads curve so sharply that the dangers of misjudging your speed become even greater. Keep an eye on the speedometer.

Good rear observation is needed when you leave the motorway, particularly if you need to take the right-hand lane on the slip road. The type of reckless driver who lunges across from the outside lane to the motorway exit at the last moment can take you by surprise, so a shoulder check, or even a lifesaver, is a good idea when you move to the right-hand lane.

On the motorway

Speed

Your speed should be a steady pace at which you and your motorcycle feel comfortable, and one which is appropriate for weather conditions and traffic density – but it should not be over 70mph.

Travelling slightly below the limit will make little difference to your journey time, and may be more relaxing if you have a long stretch on the motorway ahead of you. Travelling above the limit is

Watch your speed on the motorway. It can creep up unnoticed and judgement of braking distance can lapse.

definitely not relaxing, if only because you will have to keep watching your mirrors for an ominous blue flashing light.

It seems inevitable that Gatso cameras will be used increasingly on sections of motorway that have a bad speeding record. It is a sobering thought that any motorway user could trigger off several cameras on a single journey if speed limits are completely disregarded.

It is possible to become 'speed happy' on the motorway. Your speed can creep up unnoticed and your judgement of braking distance can lapse. A gentle swerve – perhaps just to avoid metal, rubber or rope

on the road – could become alarming simply because you attempt a manoeuvre which you would never normally contemplate at such high speed.

Some riders deliberately take a bike – maybe a new machine much more powerful than its predecessor, or a borrowed one – on to the motorway to find out how fast it will go. While a quiet motorway is definitely the safest place to become familiar with how a bike feels at speed, you must take care to increase speed gradually rather than blast straight up to the 70mph range. You need time to get the feel of a new bike – the response of the controls and differences in layout – before riding fast, and cautious use in traffic is vital to avoid the danger of sudden braking leading to a skid on an unfamiliar machine.

Concentration

On a sunny day with not much traffic you might be tempted to review your roadcraft, your bank balance or your choice at the next service area, but even in good riding conditions you must concentrate.

Motorways lack many of the features that keep your mind alert: the view tends to be monotonous, scenery is often shut out by

embankments or fences, and it is all too easy for the mind to wander. On four wheels you might get away with a second's day-dreaming. On a motorcycle you might wake up in hospital.

As an advanced rider you keep your mind interested. You turn a tiresome journey into a mobile chess game, selecting your course to anticipate traffic ahead and behind, and watching for merging vehicles at junctions.

Travelling at the safe following distance with good lane discipline demands an intelligent compromise between correct practice and expediency on a busy motorway. Here, on the M25, traffic flows are typical, with cars clustered in the outside lane, most of the drivers allowing insufficient braking distance.

Lane discipline

Maintain strict lane discipline, so that you are always in the appropriate lane for your speed and the traffic conditions, and glance in the mirrors frequently so that you are constantly aware of the relative speeds of all the vehicles around you.

Poor lane discipline, generally from car drivers, is one of the most common examples of thoughtless behaviour on motorways, and it can occasionally play its part in an accident when it forces traffic into the outside lane. Far too often on motorways you see strings of cars bunched needlessly in the outside lane.

For your own safety, ride in the centre of your lane so that motorists are not tempted to pass you in the same lane with inches to spare. Confident positioning is just as important on a motorway as on other roads.

If you come up behind a 'lane hog' who fails to move over when there is plenty of space available, do not resort to aggressive tactics. Remember that the principles of good motorcycling require you to maintain a proper braking distance, so be patient and wait for an opportunity to pass safely.

Riding in the centre of your lane discourages drivers from passing you with inches to spare.

Constrained by poor lane discipline, three IAM riders wait to make better progress, spreading their positions to fill the centre lane.

Keep your distance

The need to keep a safe distance behind the vehicle in front takes on added importance on a motorway. As the sensation of speed inevitably becomes dulled, it is all too easy to close up on the vehicle ahead so that the distance between you is

Always try to preserve a safe distance, even on a congested motorway – this behaviour at 70mph is unforgivable.

nothing like adequate in an emergency. Keep reminding yourself of this point, by checking the speedometer if it helps to bring home to you the speeds being ridden.

You are deluding yourself if you think that riding within this safe distance is acceptable because you can see several vehicles ahead. This attitude ignores all kinds of possibilities: the driver ahead might brake suddenly if faced with debris on the road, inoperative brake lights on the vehicle ahead could deny you valuable reaction time, a

vehicle from the other carriageway could crash through the central reservation, or the vehicle ahead might even suffer a tyre blow-out.

There is plenty of debris on our motorways. A thrown tyre tread, a bundle of rope or an exhaust pipe may just be an inconvenience to a car driver, but to you they can spell disaster unless seen in good time.

In dense traffic overtaking vehicles often slot into the safe gap you have left. All you can do is throttle back for a moment and drop back accordingly.

Slip road courtesy

As you approach and pass an entrance slip road, keep an eye on traffic about to join the motorway. If it is safe for you to move from the inside lane to the centre lane without worrying a

driver coming up behind, it is considerate to do so in order to make life easier for the driver joining the motorway, as well as to keep yourself out of trouble.

This forethought will be

especially appreciated by lorry drivers, who are less able to adjust their speed to blend into the traffic flow. If a slip road is very busy, this courtesy is particularly appropriate.

If it is possible, courteously moving across to the centre lane at an entrance slip road makes life easier for drivers joining the flow.

Changing lanes and overtaking

Take special care with your rear observation when planning a lane change to overtake. You should always be aware of the pattern of traffic behind you, but on occasion a lapse in concentration can make you forget about a vehicle holding station in the blind spot just behind your right shoulder. If in any doubt, make a shoulder check to supplement your mirror observation before changing course to an outer lane.

Changing lanes to overtake in heavy motorway traffic requires your best powers of observation. Frequent checking in your mirrors is needed to size up the movements of vehicles behind you, and you should take care not to compromise your safe following distance when exploiting a gap in the flow. Signal in good time and avoid making your lane change suddenly.

Many riders and drivers signal left by rote at the end of an overtaking manoeuvre. This is generally unnecessary unless you think it useful to give notice of your intentions to a driver breathing down your neck, or a driver in the inside lane who may be about to aim for the same space as you.

The heavy congestion on some motorways, for example the M25 at peak hours, means that sometimes traffic in the outer lanes will be moving more slowly than in the inner lanes. The *Highway Code* has some advice which you can take provided you apply common sense. It says, 'Do not overtake on the left unless traffic is moving slowly in queues and vehicles on the right are moving more slowly than you are.'

Provided this advice is not used for queue-hopping, on a motorcycle your higher eye level and better all-round view will allow

Overtaking on a motorway requires impeccable mirror work and good judgement of speed and distance...

Your move to the next lane should be made safely, in good time and after signalling...

After the manoeuvre, you will return to the inside lane if it is clear for a reasonable distance ahead.

you to make good progress. It is essential to keep the speed differential between your machine and the general traffic stream low. Death-defying high-speed lane filtering does nothing to improve the image of motorcycling and can only lead to an accident in the end.

Advanced checklist

- Treat the 70mph maximum as a limit, not a target that you must reach.

- Remember two essential disciplines of motorway riding: maintain a safe following distance at all times and keep in the right lane.

- Be sure not to let concentration lapse if your journey becomes monotonous.

What the examiner looks for

- Is the speed limit observed?

- Do you follow other vehicles at a safe distance?

- Are your lane discipline, positioning and rear observation to a high standard?

- Do you concentrate well?

- Do you judge speed and distance accurately, allowing you to anticipate the movements of other vehicles?

Difficult conditions and emergencies

Motorway fog

A multiple pile-up on a fogbound motorway occurs almost every winter because so many drivers travel too fast and too close together. The poor motorcyclist has little chance of escaping serious injury or death in these catastrophic accidents. As long as so much bad driving persists, the only worthwhile advice must be to avoid motorways in fog.

If you do find fog coming down while riding on a motorway, your actions should be governed by the same rules which apply to coping with fog on other roads (see pages 62-63). Reduce speed to retain a safe braking distance within your range of vision, try to keep to the inside or centre lanes, and ensure that you ride with your dipped headlight on.

Crosswinds

Since speeds are normally higher on motorways, you need to be alert to the increased effect of crosswinds, which can push your bike off course. Dropping as low on the tank as your back and hand controls will allow is your obvious response, particularly for head winds, and you soon learn to lean instinctively into a side wind to compensate for the pressure.

You must be prepared for sharply changing wind pressures at bridges, cuttings and valleys, and when passing coaches and large lorries. These vehicles work up to higher speeds on motorways, so be ready for severe turbulence – which can throw you right off course – when near them. The effect of the wind will also vary as the motorway changes direction, but this is gradual enough to be easily allowed for.

Passing a heavy lorry can subject your machine to severe turbulence.

Breakdowns on motorways

Motorway breakdowns are often caused by factors which a diligent rider can avoid. Do not push your bike beyond its limitations in age or design, and ensure that it is in the best possible condition to cope with the vibration of continuous high speed and the stresses on engine, transmission and frame.

Make sure oil level is near the maximum, as consumption often increases at high speed. Think carefully about fuel level to avoid running out between service areas, as most petrol tanks give a range of little more than 120 miles – less than two hours' riding on the motorway.

To give their best at prolonged high speeds, tyres sometimes need to be inflated a little more than normal. Our speed limits and the frequency with which riders hop on and off motorways mean that this precaution is more appropriate to riding on the continent, but the higher speeds of motorways do mean that checking the pressure and condition of your tyres becomes important. Analysis of motorway accidents has shown that one in six is caused by tyre failure, so pay good attention to your tyres.

If you are ever forced to stop on a motorway, pull over to the far left of the hard shoulder (use of the hard shoulder, of course, is permissible only in an emergency). Leave your rear light and indicator on as warning to other drivers, and either stay with your bike to wait for a police patrol vehicle or start walking to the nearest emergency telephone. Red arrows on the marker posts (at 100-metre intervals) indicate the direction of the nearest one, which will never be more than half a mile away.

If you are able to resume your journey, do not pull straight on to the main carriageway after moving off. Treat the hard shoulder as an acceleration lane, making your move to the inside lane of the motorway only when your speed matches that of the vehicles around you.

Motorway warning signals

Automatic motorway signals give you a recommended maximum speed during fog, on the approach to an incident or even during heavy rain, as well as giving warning of lane closures ahead or even the need to stop or leave the motorway in the event of a serious accident.

Temporary speed limits are used to calm congested traffic during busy periods.

Some drivers and riders ignore these signals, believing they have been left on by mistake if no obvious need for them can be seen. It is worth confirming, therefore, that the police are extremely diligent in employing these signals when they are necessary and in switching them off again as soon as danger is cleared.

Always obey them, because they invariably warn that a hazard does exist, perhaps a mile or two down the carriageway.

Recently a new type of motorway sign has been installed in many areas. It uses a matrix of lights which can spell out more detailed messages, giving advance warning of congestion, road works or accidents. The messages tend to be more up to the minute on these signs and it is as well to do as they instruct or advise.

Experiments continue into ways of dealing with congestion on motorways. At the time of writing the busiest sections of the M25 are controlled by temporary speed limits during the rush hour. Conspicuously indicated on overhead gantrys, these limits – typically 50mph or 60mph – are designed to 'calm' the traffic flow and eliminate the familiar stop-go phenomenon that occurs at peak times.

Roadworks and contraflows

At roadworks and contraflows watch out for blanked-out white lines and 'rumble strips', road debris, a poor surface on the hard shoulder and camber changes through the central reservation.

Roadworks and contraflows are a familiar part of the motorway landscape. By and large coning-off systems, lane restrictions and carriageway changes are well designed, and advance warning is normally given at least a mile ahead. But restraint and planning are needed when you approach them.

Make any lane change in good time, avoiding the late pushing and shoving into the traffic flow that you sometimes see from press-on-regardless car drivers. These tactics can trigger a train of ever-increasing braking from a row of vehicles, sometimes bringing traffic to a standstill. We have all experienced occasions when the motorway flow

inexplicably comes to a complete halt, simply because one thoughtless driver cuts in at the last moment.

Speed through contraflows is often restricted to 50mph, but the way limits are applied is not consistent throughout the country. Obey the signs you see and make sure you preserve your safe following distance when the motorway is congested.

Watch out for surface changes. Awkward cambers can be encountered where a contraflow takes you through the central reservation, blanked-out white lines and edge-of-carriageway 'rumble strips' can take you by surprise, the hard shoulder is not always smooth, and debris from road works can lie in your path. You may also find a traffic cone lying in the road because a lorry's wheels have clipped it.

Motorway hold-ups cause less frustration to motorcyclists because they can filter through, but do this safely and take care not to upset other drivers. If you display courtesy and proceed unobtrusively, the car or lorry driver ahead will often ease over to allow you to make progress. Use of the hard shoulder is illegal unless permitted by roadworks signs.

6 ADVANCED ADVICE FOR YOUR RIDING CAREER

Accidents

Stop and think

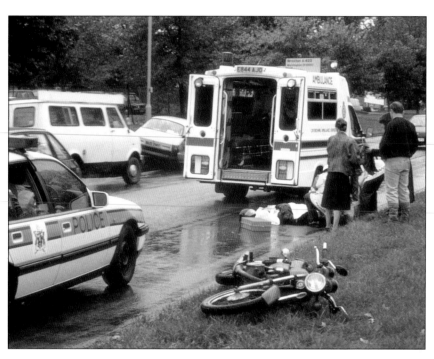

If you encounter an accident, quick thinking is necessary in order to offer all possible help before the emergency services arrive.

Everyone hopes never to be involved in a road accident, but the chances of avoiding one throughout your riding life are statistically quite small, even for an advanced motorcyclist. It is worth taking a little trouble, therefore, to learn what to do if the worst does occur. Sooner or later you are also likely to arrive at someone else's accident.

Many things have to be done at once at an accident, and there is more involved than merely helping the casualties. You must warn other drivers, send for help, and protect the site from further accidents until the emergency services arrive. Your actions in these first few minutes could be a matter of life and death. Think about what you do: people who are injured and unable to move could be more seriously hurt if you try to pull them out of a crashed car.

Do not park your motorcycle where it could be a hazard to other traffic. The best place to park is at the roadside where it can be spotted easily by approaching traffic. When it is dark, position your bike so that its headlight illuminates the scene of the accident, but also so that it can still be seen by approaching drivers.

Switch off the engine on a crashed vehicle or motorcycle; apply a vehicle's handbrake and chock the wheels if this seems necessary. Make sure that no-one in the vicinity of the accident is smoking.

Approaching drivers need plenty of time and distance to slow down and stop, or negotiate the accident. Run back along the side of the road for at least 100 metres, or until the accident is going out of view. Make a clear 'slow down' signal by moving your arm vigorously up and down, with palm face down, as if pressing down repeatedly on a heavy weight, and point decisively to the accident scene. On bends it may be useful to recruit a second person to give advance warning.

Someone should stand near the site and guide vehicles round the accident. Stand in the headlights of a car or under a streetlamp at night, and remember that it will help to wear a pale or reflective garment. Hold a white handkerchief, or better still a torch, to draw extra attention to yourself.

Summoning help

Your first priority is to send for help. If this means leaving casualties unattended, get someone else to telephone the emergency services. If no-one else is around, you must do this.

When you dial 999 it is vital to provide precise information for the emergency services. Work out your answers to the essential questions. What is the exact location (look for an obvious landmark if you do not know)? How many casualties are there and how serious are their injuries? Are the casualties trapped? Is the accident causing danger? How many vehicles are involved? Are they cars? Lorries? Tankers? Buses or coaches? Is a traffic jam developing? Are petrol or chemicals spilling?

Tell the operator your telephone number and ask for

Dialling 999 is the first priority if emergency assistance is required. Police, ambulance or fire brigade – or even all three – may be needed, and very precise information must be given.

ambulance, police or fire brigade; you will be connected to each in turn if all three are required. Ask for Ambulance if there are casualties. Ask for Police if there are casualties, danger or obstruction to traffic.

Ask for Fire Brigade if people are trapped, if petrol or chemicals have spilled over the road, or if there is risk of fire.

After telephoning return to the accident scene to help with the casualties or traffic.

Helping casualties

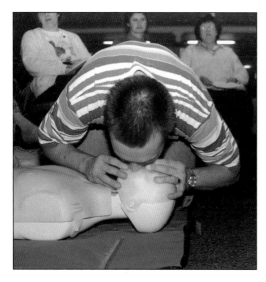

Basic first aid training is invaluable. Attempt mouth-to-mouth resuscitation if you cannot detect breathing.

Only move injured people if there is immediate danger, since you could aggravate internal, back or neck injuries. Make sure the person can breathe. Inspect the inside of the mouth and back of the throat. To avoid the danger of choking, remove any food, sweets or false teeth. If you cannot detect breathing, attempt mouth-to-mouth resuscitation.

Place the casualty on his or her back, and support the neck so the head falls back to open the airway. Pinch the nose shut and hold the mouth open. Cover the mouth with yours, and blow firmly to inflate the lungs. Then release the nose and mouth. Keep repeating the procedure until the casualty starts to breathe spontaneously.

If unconscious, move the casualty gently into the recovery position to avoid choking on the tongue or gorging. This involves turning the casualty's body gently on its side and bending arms and legs to maintain this position. Turn the head to one side, facing slightly downwards.

If there is serious bleeding, apply firm pressure to the bleeding point to stem the flow of blood. Use a pad or apply a sterile dressing and bandage firmly. Look for limb fractures and try to stop these limbs moving. If injured people are sitting up and in no immediate danger, do not make them leave the car. Leave them where they are and support their heads to minimise the possibility of them passing out and choking.

Keep all casualties warm, including shock cases, but do not give them any pain relievers, alcohol, other drinks, food or cigarettes – they may have internal injuries and need operations.

If you are not sure what to do, leave casualties alone provided they are breathing and not bleeding heavily.

Helmet removal

There is considerable controversy over the need to remove the helmet of an injured motorcyclist, but there is a simple guideline that any rider would like to see observed if an injury occurs.

If the rider is breathing and there is no danger of choking, leave the helmet on. If the rider is unconscious and is clearly not breathing, the brain will start to die within four minutes from oxygen starvation. The stark choice is then made for you. Would

Study the technique for removing a full-face helmet safely, without causing further injury to the rider.

you prefer to try to preserve life or just stand by? If the following advice is used for safe helmet removal, you will minimise the risk of further injury.

Unfasten the chin strap before you attempt to remove the helmet. Most UK straps are of the D-ring type, but there are others with a fastener that works like a seat belt buckle, with a catch that must be pressed to release the strap. The BMW System helmet, as used by some police forces and many civilian riders, has a hinge-up front section released by pressing a button on each side of the chin piece. If this section can be raised, the main helmet can be left undisturbed.

Two people are needed to remove a full-face helmet safely. One supports the head and neck, the other lifts the helmet. Move the helmet backwards and lift it until it is free of the chin. Then move it forwards, so that it clears the base of the skull, and lift it straight off. The head and neck must remain supported until a surgical collar is fitted, otherwise serious injury could result.

Fire

There is just one set of accident circumstances when you should break the rule and pull injured people from their vehicles. Although fire occurs in only a tiny proportion of road accidents, it requires instant action and great presence of mind.

The fire may be caused by a short circuit from damaged wiring, in which case you should have plenty of time to deal with it as long as petrol is not seeping from a ruptured tank dangerously near it. If one of the crashed vehicles carries a fire extinguisher, aim it at the seat of the fire and keep up the discharge until the flames are out.

If the fire is in the engine bay, opening the bonnet can feed the fire with a draught of air, causing the flames to flare up. If you can, open the bonnet just enough to allow you to aim the fire extinguisher inside, but only if you can identify with certainty the source of the flames. If you cannot see where the fire is coming from before you open the bonnet a fraction, open it wide and be ready to act quickly if the fire expands. If

you can, break the electrical circuit feeding the fire by disconnecting the battery leads.

Many electronic devices used on cars and motorcycles are encapsulated in fluoro-carbon plastics. These are perfectly safe in normal use, but if subject to fire they can generate hydrofluoric acid residues which are so exceedingly dangerous when handled that amputation is the only medical solution possible with current knowledge.

A petrol fire is even more serious, calling for heroic action if anything is to be done to save people trapped inside the car. A petrol fire can often be avoided, however, by making sure there is no possibility of any sparks near the damaged car. No-one must smoke, people in nailed shoes should keep clear and no attempt should be made by anyone but the emergency services to cut away metal to release occupants. Petrol cannot set itself alight, so one of your first actions must be to switch off the car's ignition to avoid the possibility of any sparks in the vicinity.

Riding abroad

Hints and tips

Riding abroad always demands extra care but as an advanced motorcyclist you should be able to take it all in your stride. Here are a few pointers.

When riding abroad, enjoy your journey and avoid setting unmanageable daily targets.

• Concentrate hard on the job in hand – not just at first (that comes automatically) but even after you have a few hundred kilometres under your belt.

• Most 'riding on the wrong side' incidents occur when you are relaxed, especially if you have parked on the opposite (left) side of the road and there is no other traffic about. Take special care when leaving filling stations, shops or laybys.

• If you think it will help, stick a 'Ride on the Right' message on the instrument panel.

• Continental traffic laws by and large equate to ours, but they are often enforced with great firmness – and being a visiting tourist may not get you off the hook. For example, French *autoroute* police can

impose on-the-spot fines for speeding, payable in cash, travellers' cheques or by major credit card. Cannot pay? Then they may impound your bike until you can. Remember they can calculate your average speed between toll booths and issue a ticket on this evidence alone.

• Keep to other rules too. 'Stop' signs mean just that, and if you roll across one you might just find a police officer waiting to step out and catch you.

• It is compulsory to ride with the headlight on, day and night, in some European countries.

• Watch out for continuing use of the 'priority to the right' rule in France. Unless there are signs or road markings to the contrary, drivers approaching from your right at junctions may emerge unexpectedly. Many French people have lived by this rule throughout their driving lives and sometimes still stick to it, although the French authorities have generally brought their practice into line with the rest of Europe. Particular care is needed in towns.

• At traffic lights you will often encounter a continually flashing amber light. It means you should cross the junction with great caution and be prepared to give way.

• A speeding offence is the most common reason for being stopped, so make sure you know the limits in each country you enter.

• Keep a special eye out for cyclists, especially in Holland, Belgium and Denmark. Local custom, as well as the law, expects cyclists to be treated with courtesy and consideration – unlike the treatment they often get in Britain. Often they have right of way where a cycle track crosses a road.

• Take great care with tram lines and do not argue with trams. They usually have priority.

• Do not set yourself unmanageable daily mileages. Fatigue sets in easily on long motorway runs and drowsiness can be heightened by a big midday meal. Take it easy, enjoy yourself and let your passenger (if you carry one) enjoy the journey too.

• Buy a good road atlas and plan your route properly. If you are in no rush choose quiet roads.

• Do not forget to find out if you need a Green Card or a Bail Bond for the country you are visiting. For certain countries you will need an International Driving Licence.

The rider of a Pan-European Honda stops to enjoy the distant view of an Alpine peak.

Resuming a journey on a quiet road after a break is the classic moment for pulling away on the wrong side of the road.

Pillion passengers and sidecars

Pillion passengers

An experienced passenger rests hands on knees, balancing with the leg muscles and good body positioning.

Plenty of motorcyclists have mixed feelings about carrying passengers. Riding with a frightened, inexperienced person behind you can be irritating, even dangerous.

Passengers with no feel for motorcycling will automatically lean the wrong way when you bank your bike into a corner; they may make sudden movements which will cause the steering to wobble when riding in a straight line; they will grab your waist when accelerating and then slide forwards when braking, pushing you on to the fuel tank. After dismounting they may even say they enjoyed the ride and would love to do it again…

Experienced pillion passengers, however, have as good a feel as the rider for motorcycling. They know how to behave unobtrusively and helpfully on the road, and they provide the pleasures of good company and shared experiences at the end of an enjoyable day.

The advice which follows should help to turn the first type of pillion passenger into the second, so that you can ride more safely as well as increase your enjoyment of motorcycling by sharing the pleasure.

You must first remind your novice passenger that motorcycling is like riding a bike, explaining that bends are negotiated by leaning the bike over, not by steering the front wheel. Describe how sudden movements affect your control of the bike, explaining that your passenger's body must remain in line with yours at all times, even if uncertainty is felt about the angles involved through bends. Your passenger's feet must always remain on the foot-rests, which means resisting the temptation to put feet on the ground when the bike is coming to a stop.

Some riders like their passenger to use the rear hand rail that is often part of the bike's dual seat design, but it is better for an inexperienced passenger to hold the rider around the waist or by the belt if the rider's suit has one. This will minimise changes in weight distribution under acceleration and braking, until your passenger gets used to the way you ride.

You can explain that many pillion riders, once they have some experience, rest their hands on their knees and maintain equilibrium with their leg muscles and good body positioning, gripping the rear bar or saddle only when you brake heavily or accelerate briskly.

It is difficult to talk to each other on the move, so arrange a simple signalling system. Make it clear that the best way for your passenger to tell you to stop is with a firm tap on the shoulder.

Before setting off, make sure your passenger's helmet is fastened securely and comfortably, and ask your companion to get on the bike after you so that you can keep things steady and claim a good share of the dual saddle. Ensure your passenger is comfortable

and has found the foot-rests before you move off.

Never accelerate too quickly, as a newcomer to motorcycling will be far more frightened than impressed. Even with an experienced passenger, ride with more restraint than usual and try to avoid sudden changes in speed and course. Remember that your passenger's view of the road will be obscured, giving little chance to anticipate and prepare for sudden movements.

Until sensitivity to motorcycling is acquired, it is best for a novice passenger to hold the rider around the waist.

Intercom and bike-to-bike radios

BMW System 3 helmet and Sonic radio.

It is now established practice for the Government motorcycle test to be conducted with a one-way radio operated by the examiner. This means that many riders have already experienced the convenience of receiving route instructions and observations, and there is an increasing trend to the use of two-way radios, especially for touring.

A rider-to-passenger intercom set, such as a Sonic or Autocom, offers great benefits. As well as being able to talk to the rider on a long journey, the passenger can take on the task of map-reading and route-finding. Intercoms are also a valuable training aid, and experienced IAM observers use them to give commentary rides to test candidates.

Bike-to-bike intercom sets, however, can be a mixed blessing, apart from being expensive. Concern has been expressed about the correct use of vocabulary between riders, so that, for example, 'No' is not misheard as 'Go'. There is also the danger of less experienced riders being given instructions which may lead them into trouble. If you decide to invest in bike-to-bike equipment, make sure you establish clear rules for its use before you take to the road. Some of the best designs have built-in noise suppression that allows clear communication even at high speeds.

Sidecars

Motorcycling can be addictive! The fact that young riders find it difficult to sacrifice their motorcycling if they start a family is the traditional reason for the existence of sidecar combinations. Determination to continue riding leads them to overlook the inherent design and safety disadvantages of adding a

BMW K100 with Hurlingham sidecar.

single-wheeled weight to one side of a motorcycle, but many claim to enjoy what has been described as 'doing the impossible with the unrideable'.

Although sidecars are not often seen these days, a few specialists remain to cater for the needs of those who want to stick with motorcycling at all costs. A complete appraisal of this difficult aspect of motorcycling is beyond the purpose of this book, but some basic points can be made.

The geometry of a motorcycle and sidecar is a poor compromise for cornering, since the wheels cannot all follow a constant radius, and the wildly uneven weight and power distribution compound the problems. The basic difference is that you have to steer through corners, not bank through them.

The basic rule for cornering with a sidecar mounted on the left is to apply power through left-handers (where the sidecar tries to lift off the ground) and remove power through right-handers. The fact that braking encourages the sidecar to overtake the bike (unless the sidecar has its own brake to offset this effect) produces a tendency to turn right, which must be countered by steering gently to the left. Acceleration produces an opposite tendency to turn left, which must be countered by steering gently to the right.

These characteristics are minimised by paying careful attention to the position of the sidecar wheel in relation to the motorcycle's rear wheel, the attachment point positions, angle of lean, front fork angles and spring travel. Even so, the best designs will have shortcomings in fast, bumpy corners.

Specialists have developed a niche in the market for three-wheel enthusiasts and can give advice. They know the modifications required to most large-capacity machines – such as BMW K100, Kawasaki GPZ1100 or Yamaha TR1 Vee-twin – to make them suitable for adaptation.

Advanced checklist

- Make sure you give sensible advice to inexperienced pillion riders so that they know what to do and travel without fear.

- A passenger who leans the wrong way, makes sudden movements and slides back and forth with acceleration and braking can impair your control of your machine.

- Even with an experienced passenger, ride with additional restraint; try to avoid sudden changes in speed and course.

- The safe handling of a motorcycle and sidecar requires practice: absorb the special techniques described here for cornering, braking and accelerating.

7 THE ADVANCED MOTORCYCLING TEST

What the test involves

Why you should take the Advanced Motorcycling Test

Just how good a rider are you? The most experienced motorcyclist is one who never stops learning, for road conditions are continuously evolving and you need to practise your skills no matter how expert you may become.

You must remember that the Government L-test is only a very basic, elementary examination. The real learning starts when you can throw away your L-plates and begin the acquisition of mature riding skills. Many riders realise this, and there comes a time when they want to reassure themselves that their skills are developing along the right lines.

This is why the Institute of Advanced Motorists exists. It was founded in 1956 as a non-profit making organisation and is registered as a charity. It is dedicated to the promotion of road safety by encouraging motorists and motorcyclists to take pride in good driving and riding. By taking the IAM's test, you can measure the progress you have made since passing the basic test. The motto of the IAM is 'skill with responsibility'.

The Advanced Motorcycling Test was introduced in 1976 and has proved very popular among riders. It has been acclaimed by the motorcycle press, by experienced riders of all ages, by road safety officials and by motorcycle clubs. Well over 300,000 motorcycling and driving tests have so far been carried out, and 79 per cent of the motorcyclists who have taken the test have passed and become members of the IAM.

Over 500 companies have used the driving test to improve the skills of staff using company-owned vehicles, leading to reduced accident rates and lower insurance costs.

If every driver and motorcyclist had the enthusiasm to pass the IAM test and the self-discipline to apply high standards all the time, there would be a dramatic fall in the casualties on British roads. Human error causes 95 per cent of road accidents.

Preparing for the test

The IAM has over 300 Groups around the country and overseas, and of these 60 are dedicated to members with motorcycling interests. Groups have schemes to advise prospective candidates on preparing for the test, and these are especially recommended to candidates who wish to find out more about advanced riding. Two out of three who apply for the test come via the Groups and the pass rate for riders who choose this route is over 90 per cent.

The approaches vary from informal classroom sessions to on-the-road advice from skilled and experienced IAM members who belong to observer teams. Very often these teams have the benefit of tuition from class one police riders who are themselves

An IAM Group tutor watches a rider perfecting a figure-of-eight manoeuvre in a car park.

You can benefit from the exceptional roadcraft of class one police riders if you participate in IAM Group training.

Group members, so one can expect a high degree of expertise. If you like the idea of joining a club whose main interest is in advanced riding, contact with your local Group should be your first move.

The well-established commercial training organisations mainly cater for Compulsory Basic Training but some offer advanced courses, although they tend to be

expensive compared with Group participation.

Some experienced riders pass the test without specific preparation. Studying all the guidance in this book and applying it every time you ride should enable you to pass without too much difficulty.

You can apply to take the Advanced Motorcycling Test by contacting the IAM at the address on page 80.

The test format

A typical test takes 90 minutes and covers around 35 miles. The route incorporates all kinds of road conditions, including motorways (if there is one within reach), dual-carriageways, congested urban areas, main

circumstances permit – progress with safety. You may be asked to carry out certain manoeuvres at low speeds on a course through markers on an off-road site.

There are no trick questions and no attempts to catch you out. Throughout the test the examiner will follow you on another machine, giving you route instructions by bike-to-bike intercom or stopping at intervals. This is the 'pursuit' method used by the police for their own test. It has been found to be by far the most efficient way of maintaining a prolonged check on a rider's behaviour on the road.

The examiner, who will always be the holder of a police class one certificate and have a traffic patrol background, will tell you whether you have passed or failed at the end of the test. There may be praise, and certainly constructive criticism will be offered even if your standard of riding is good enough to pass. The test is conducted in a spirit of friendliness, not intimidation.

Occasionally the examiner will identify a potentially

Infringements of the law, such as neglecting to halt and put a foot down at a 'stop' sign, will result in failure.

dangerous fault. A quiet word will help you to correct it. You will not be failed for minor faults, but infringements of the law cannot be condoned and will result in failure.

Who and where?

Anyone with a full UK licence can take the test provided he or she has not been convicted of a serious traffic offence in the last three years. You can take the test on almost any motorcycle which you provide yourself, as long as it has sufficient power to sustain 70mph where required.

You will not have to travel far to take the test – the IAM has a network of over 130 test routes nationwide. The examiner will fix a mutually acceptable date and time, and will meet you at a pre-arranged rendezvous.

The Advanced Motorcycling Test is conducted in a spirit of friendliness, not intimidation.

roads, narrow country lanes and residential streets.

You are not expected to give a display of fancy riding: you should handle your machine in the steady, workmanlike way in which you ride every day. The examiners do not, for example, expect exaggeratedly slow speeds or excessive signalling. They want to see you ride with due regard for road, traffic and weather conditions, observing all speed limits. They want to see you riding briskly and showing that you are not afraid to cruise at the legal limit when

After the test

The duty to set an example

As a member of the Institute of Advanced Motorists, your conduct on the road will make you an ambassador for motorcycling. Try to improve your skills and keep analysing your riding to make sure you are not slipping into bad habits. You may consider repeating the Advanced Motorcycling Test every few years in order to sharpen your skills.

Benefits of IAM membership

When you pass the Advanced Motorcycling Test and become a member of the Institute of Advanced Motorists, a few of the many benefits available to you include:

- **Badge** The right to display the IAM's badge and certificate, providing visible proof of the high standards that you have achieved.

- **Insurance** An introduction to insurers who may give special terms – the discount can be as much as 20 per cent – subject to a satisfactory proposal.

- **Magazine** A magazine, *Milestones*, which is published every four months. It is produced for IAM members and written by people who take a keen interest in motoring and motorcycling.

- **Social activities** The chance to meet other men and women who share your outlook on motorcycling. You can decide to join one of the IAM Groups and take part in the events they organise.

- **Discounts** These are available from a range of organisations, including Green Flag National Breakdown and the RAC.

IAM benefits include discounted membership of Green Flag National Breakdown.

INSTITUTE OF ADVANCED MOTORISTS

IAM House
359 Chiswick High Road
London W4 4HS

Tel 0181 994 4403
(24-hour answering service)

Fax 0181 994 9249